# pipes

## god's spiritual gifts
## flowing through you

### william clay smith

# Table of Contents

# CHAPTER 1

# What Flows Through You?

It was the dry season. My mother was praying for rain. We had young orange trees set out that will die if they didn't get water soon. These were not orange trees in our yard, they were in our grove. They were our income, they were our future. My father had passed away three years earlier, and now it was up to my mother to take care of all our groves. I was only five, but something in her prayers told me this was a critical moment.

My aunts owned a grove nearby – the Estate Grove. They had a deep well that pumped thousands of gallons of water. In those days, aluminum pipes were laid from the well to each row of trees, and connected with sprinkler pipes that had tiny holes in them. Millions of drops of life-giving water poured from those holes and kept the groves alive.

The answer to our problem was a few feet hundred feet away. All we needed was for the pipes to bring the water to us.

I look at this world and see many dry souls. They have signs of life. With the right care, these souls could flourish. They could throw off disease, hurt, and loneliness. These souls could live. But they do not.

The frustrating part is seeing the life-giving water they need. It's in the lives of normal people, who decided to follow Jesus. They have drawn the life-giving water from Jesus; they are thriving. But they have decided to keep the water for themselves. They become puddles, sometimes ponds. They never see themselves as a pipe.

A few people do. They channel the life-giving water of Jesus down a row or two. Souls flourish. Life happens. People grow healthy.

What would happen if every Jesus follower saw themselves as a pipe?

A two year old might whisper into your ear that she loves Jesus. Hurts and pains might find not just a listening ear, but a caring heart. Hands might reach out and build a wheelchair ramp. A lesson you teach might direct a person to make a life changing decision.

Your life is not an accident. You are not a random product of biologic function. You are a gift to this world from God, fashioned and shaped uniquely for a reason. You were placed in time and space so the world could receive something from you. You are a pipe.

When you listen to Jesus, when you follow him, he will invite you to point your life toward specific people in specific times and places. Then he will pour himself through you. You will bring hope. You will bring truth. You will bring grace. You will solve problems. You will introduce people to living water, the living water of Jesus. You will be a pipe.

That's what this book is about. I want to help you discover the thrill of Jesus flowing through you, so someone else is blessed. I want you to have the adventure of pouring out Jesus inside you onto dry souls.

I want you to find out life is more than tasks; it is living each moment with an awareness that you can bless people because Jesus is in you.

## Why People Never Let Jesus Flow

I remember in that dry time a neighbor had aluminum pipes that he didn't use anymore. He had installed overhead irrigation in his grove. So acutely did I feel my mother's anxiety, I asked her why we didn't ask him for the pipes. She told me, "I did. He said he might need them." Though I was a child, I remember thinking, "That doesn't make sense."

Why would people, who had the capability to meet a need, decide not to use their lives to let Jesus flow through them?

People choose to remain immature. They believe life is all about their wants and needs. A child-like greed holds sway over their decisions, so they cannot let go of time, energy, or resources. They believe if they let something flow through them to another person, they lose.

People remain trapped by their wounds. They see themselves as victims. A deep sense of unworthiness keeps them from seeing the gifts they have to share. Sometimes they fall in love with their hurt, because it keeps them in a position of consuming instead of giving.

People never let Jesus flow because they know it will change their lives – and they see that change as a threat. If they embrace a calling to pipe the water of Jesus to dry souls, they will have to change their schedules, their priorities, and their allocation of resources. They know their world will move around and they like their world the way it is.

The main reason people do not want to let Jesus flow through them, is life will not be about them. No one gives glory to a pipe. Most of us only pay attention to pipes when they clog or break. We're interested in the water. In our self-centeredness, we can't stand for the attention to be off of us. We want the water for ourselves, but we don't want to pipe it to others.

There is one more reason people don't pipe the water of Jesus to dry souls: they don't have it. The real tragedy of these people is they sometimes will even do the work of laying out their lives to dry souls. The dry souls perk up with hope. But the connection to the well is not there. Because so much water is being pumped out of the well, some will trickle down the pipe. But there is no force, no consistency, no volume. If you aren't connected to Jesus, you can't bring what people ultimately need.

Connecting to Jesus happens when you choose to follow him, not for a moment, but forever. You connect to Jesus by asking him to forgive you and to take control of your life. It is an eternal decision and a daily choice. It has nothing to do with religion and everything to do with relationship. Connecting to Jesus is the decision to help you discover why on earth you are here.

## Why God Made You

God designed us to do something beyond ourselves. He commanded the first man and woman to "[28]Be fruitful and increase in number; fill the earth and subdue it. Rule over the fish in the sea and the bird in the sky and over every living creature that moves on the ground."[1] Our purpose is beyond ourselves. God tasks us with the idea of being fruitful – to pour our lives into children and family. Take hold of the space we are given and subdue it; rule over it. People may argue over

---

1 Genesis 1:28.

the particulars of this God-given purpose, but our purpose is beyond ourselves.

If you do not follow Jesus, you will never find your purpose. This book is for people who have made that decision. Following Jesus means discovering the mission he specifically has for you. When a person joins the Jesus movement, they are given gifts. In church world, we call them "spiritual gifts," because they come from the Holy Spirit: "There are different kinds of gifts, but the same Spirit distributes them."[2] I know this sounds obvious, but spiritual gifts are used for spiritual purposes. These gifts provide God sized energy and intervention to spiritually dry people. While everyone on the planet has the potential to have this gifting from the Spirit, the gifts are not given until a person makes the commitment to follow Jesus. The water is gushing, but until you are connected to Jesus, the gifts are not flowing.

How do you know what spiritual gifts are yours? The best way to discover your gifts is experience. Try something. If you experience frustration, lack of fruit, or a sense of moving farther away from God, you may be trying to channel something that simply isn't there. Spiritual gifts are discovered, not ordered.

## What are Spiritual Gifts?

The New Testament does not give us a single comprehensive listing of spiritual gifts. Most scholars agree that the passages that address spiritual gifts are to provide illustrations of how God gifts people. There is debate about whether there are spiritual gifts beyond those mentioned in scripture; but these debates do not help people discover

---

2   1 Corinthians 12:4.

God's purpose for their lives. That's my goal: not to debate about the gifts, but to help you find your gifts.

There are five scripture passages that directly address spiritual gifts.

In 1 Corinthians 12:7-10, nine gifts are mentioned:

> [7] Now to each one the manifestation of the Spirit is given for the common good. [8] To one there is given through the Spirit a message of *wisdom*, to another a message of *knowledge* by means of the same Spirit, [9] to another *faith* by the same Spirit, to another gifts of *healing* by that one Spirit, [10] to another *miraculous powers*, to another **prophecy**, to another distinguishing between *spirits*, to another *speaking in different kinds of tongues*, and to still another the *interpretation of tongues* (italics added).

In the same chapter, in verse 28, Paul again provides a list:

> [28] And God has placed in the church first of all *apostles*, second *prophets*, third *teachers*, then *miracles*, then gifts of *healing*, of *helping*, of *guidance*, and *of different kinds of tongues* (italics added).

Note the difference in the two lists. Addressing a specific group of believers, Paul does not give an exhaustive list, but suggestive lists. Gifts of healing, miracles/wondrous works, and tongues are mentioned in both lists; other significant gifts are not.

To Jesus followers in Ephesus, Paul gives another different listing, with some overlap in Ephesians 4:11-12:

> [11] So Christ himself gave the *apostles*, the *prophets*, the *evangelists*, the *pastors* and *teachers*, [12] to equip his people for works of service, so that the body of Christ may be built up (italics added).

In this listing, there is no mention of miracles or tongues; however, apostles, prophets, and teachers are.

1st Peter 4:10-11 briefly mentions spiritual gifts, although the focus is more on giving Jesus glory in his church:

> [10] Each of you should use whatever gift you have received to serve others, as faithful stewards of God's grace in its various forms. [11] *If anyone speaks*, they should do so as one who speaks the very words of God. *If anyone serves*, they should do so with the strength God provides, so that in all things God may be praised through Jesus Christ. To him be the glory and the power for ever and ever. Amen (italics added).

Finally, Paul offers a listing in Romans 12:6-8:

> [6] We have different gifts, according to the grace given to each of us. If your gift is *prophesying*, then prophesy in accordance with your faith; [7] if it is *serving*, then serve; if it is *teaching*, then teach; [8] if it is to *encourage*, then give encouragement; if it is *giving*, then give generously; if it is to *lead,* do it diligently; if it is to *show mercy,* do it cheerfully (italics added).

This listing incorporates gifts from all the other lists. This suggests the list is offered as broad categories. Indeed, all the other gifts can be reasonably included under the heading of these gifts. To me, this passage provides a helpful outline we will follow. I think you discover your gifts in one or more of these categories:

Prophesy
Serving
Teaching
Encouragement
Giving
Leadership
Mercy

## Gifts From Grace

All the water pumping out of the well in the middle of the grove is grace. We didn't buy that water. It was there, stored in a vast underground aquifer. The water we need for life is there – free of charge.

All spiritual gifts are gifts of grace. We've done nothing to deserve them. God, who loves us, wants us to feel purposeful. He wants us to know his joy of creation and meaning. In addition to saving us by grace, he gives our lives meaning by providing a gift we can use to share his story of grace with someone else.

All the gifts you have are reasons to be grateful. If you have a heart to preach, be thankful. If you have a heart to serve, be thankful. If you have heart to teach, be thankful. If you have a heart that encourages, be thankful. If you have a heart that gives, be thankful. If you have a heart that wants to lead, be thankful. If you have a heart that gives mercy, be thankful. God gives you ability beyond yourself. You didn't earn it. Your gifts are from his free, great grace.

Being self-centered humans, we quickly start to compare our gifts to the gifts of our neighbors. If they are gifted with the same gifts we have, we are quick to be envious. We want our gifts to be in like proportion to theirs.

Trusting God means we trust him with the reach of our gifts. I envy some of my classmates from seminary who have the same gift mix that I have. But their lives are impacting more people. They are well known. They are making more money! Why hasn't God let my gifts be used in the same proportion as my classmates?

It may relate to faith. Paul says in Romans 12:6: "⁶We have different gifts, according to the grace given to each of us. If your gift is prophesying, then prophesy in accordance with your faith." The gifts I receive are given by God's grace. My faith, however, energizes the gifts.

If you are a pipe of God's grace, your faith is determining the size of your pipe. The well of God's grace may be pumping out 50,000 gallons a minute; but if your faith is small, you may only be able to receive 100 gallons a minute.

How then do you increase your faith? In the Psalms, God's people would sing prayers about what God had done, as in Psalm 106. The story of God's people is recited as a reminder to fully follow Him. Faith increases when you remember what God has already done. His past performance is the best indicator of His future behavior.

Faith is increased when it is supported in prayer. Conversations with God help us to off load our guilt and burdens, which are faith inhibitors. Make sure in prayer you are asking God to increase your faith, just as the father of the epileptic boy did in Mark 9:24: "²⁴...I believe, help my unbelief!" Confess to God your fears about using your gift. Ask him for boldness and courage.

Faith is increased when it is supported by study. Even a casual reading of the Bible will show the ordinariness of the great Biblical heroes. Men like Abraham, Moses, and David dealt with the same pressures and temptations we do. Women like Sarah, Miriam, Ruth, and Mary dealt with the same fears and anxieties we do. Their stories are in the Bible to show what an extra-ordinary God can do with ordinary people.

Faith is increased with obedience. When we obey God, it is the equivalent of working the "obedience" muscle of our souls. Our faith increases because we have followed our leader and now we are ready for greater opportunities.

Faith is increased with risk. When Jesus told the parable of the talents, he helped us to see that our God is risk tolerant. Three servants were given funds by a master. Two put the funds at risk and prospered. They were praised as "good and faithful servants." The third servant was risk adverse – he put the money in the ground, and presented it back as it was. He was condemned for his uselessness.[3] When you risk, you trust. When you trust, your faith grows.

We may not have the reach of our peers with similar gifts because God has a specific mission for us where we are. Our perspective is vastly different than God's. While we might see a friend whose gifts allow them to shine, God sees the impact that will be made by the one person we pour into. Our definitions of fame and success are limited by time. God's hall of fame of faith in Hebrews 11 features people who

---

3  Matthew 25:14-30.

were overlooked and unknown by most of the world in the time they lived.

There is also an odd dance of talent and spiritual gifts. A talent is not a gift. For example a person may be able to sing, but have no spiritual gift that enables them to encourage people in worship. You may be a talented electrician, but if you lack the gift of service, you lack the power to use that skill for Jesus' church (bad pun, but irresistible).

I've seen this more times than I count. The person gifted to teach can also cook, so we put them in the kitchen. The carpenter who is a great giver is tasked to do all the church repair jobs. The person with mercy is put on the Stewardship team. Ironically, talent often causes people to be misplaced in ministry. We pay more attention to the talent than to the spiritual gift. Talent wedded to a gift is a powerful accelerant. But never forget that giftedness trumps talent when it comes to bringing the presence of Jesus.

Your gifts and mine are given by grace. The gift is not about us. We are bodies carrying "earthen treasures."[4]

## Gift Envy

Imagine a straight pipe saying to a 90° elbow, "I wish I could be like you and turn." Imagine a pipe end plug saying to a valve section, "I would love to stop water like you." Just imagining pipes having a conversation is a little weird.

Paul plays out this conversation in 1 Corinthians 12. He tells of an imaginary conversation between eyes and ears, each telling the other,

---

4   2 Corinthians 4:7.

"I don't need you." How silly would it be if the head and feet got into an argument about which was more important. Just imagining body parts having a conversation is a little strange.

Now imagine how silly it is for one Jesus follower to say to another Jesus follower, "I wish I could teach like you." Imagine how foolish it sounds for one of Jesus' followers to say to himself or herself, "I only have the gift of service. It's really not very important, like the gift of prophecy." Imagine how ridiculous it is for a Jesus follower to envy someone else's gift.

Gift envy is nothing new. In Acts 8 a recent convert named Simon sees Peter and John laying hands on new believers; the new believers would then receive the Holy Spirit. He offers to pay Peter and John if they would give him this same power. Peter's answer in verse 8:20-22 is a warning to all of us:

> [20] Peter answered: "May your money perish with you, because you thought you could buy the gift of God with money! [21] You have no part or share in this ministry, because your heart is not right before God. [22] Repent of this wickedness and pray to the Lord in the hope that he may forgive you for having such a thought in your heart.

Envying someone else's gift is a waste of energy. You begin to believe it is about you, the pipe. It's really about the water you carry – Jesus.

## The Call

In the chapters ahead, I'll talk about each category of spiritual gifts. Whatever gifts you have, there is specific time and space for you to apply your gifts. We can loosely think of this as a "call."

The call to use your gift can come in a brief moment. I have the gift of prophesy, which is insight into the ways of God. On a recent plane trip, my wife struck up a conversation with our row mate. At first, it was the general conversation between two women at a similar place in life. I was trying to read the paper, but I kept getting drawn into the conversation. I couldn't help but notice the woman referencing prayer, church, and faith. There was a whisper from God telling me to put down the paper and pay attention to the conversation. She unfolded her story, revealing that she and her husband had recently moved to a city in our state. As our plane touched down, I sensed a call to ask if she had found a church in her new city. She said they had not, and had no idea where to look. I knew several churches and pastors near her new home and shared those names with her. She thanked me, and said she was relieved to have a place to start. My call was to serve for just a few minutes, and to be a pipe to a thirsty soul in a new city.

The call to use your gift can be a call to pick up and move for a long period of time. One family in our church, Scott and Tonya Shipes had a call like this. Scott was a rising star in his company. He had the spiritual gifts of leadership and service. I traveled with him on a mission trip to Botswana. During that trip, God spoke to Scott, and called him to leave the states and go to Botswana for three years to serve as Children's Ministry Missionary. His spiritual gifts were a perfect fit for this new calling. After serving for three years, Scott and Tonya had transformed dozens of churches in Southern Africa.

The season of your calling can be for a few minutes – like my encounter on the plane; or can be for years – like Scott and Tonya's calling to go to Africa.

How do you know when you are called? You have an unshakable burden. You have to put something aside. You feel led to a growth edge of discomfort. I believe a sure sign of a calling is a thought or two of doubt. Stepping out to answer a call is a shaky faith step. But when you do, you are being the pipe that God made you to be; and you are widening your capacity to carry his grace.

## The Rest of the Pipe Story

In that awful drought, my uncles got together, re-laid the pipe from the Estate Grove well, and borrowed pipe from some other neighbors. I remember my mother's gratitude as pipes brought that life giving water to orange trees already wilting from lack of moisture. The fruit would hold, there would be a crop, and we could hold on one more year. I was playing in the water, but the trees were drinking in life.

I've never forgotten what a pipe with cool water can mean to someone who is losing hope. If you are a follower of Jesus, you have access to life giving water. There are wilting souls who are thirsty for what you can bring. It is time for you to make sure you are connected to Jesus, and be the pipe he made you to be.

# CHAPTER 2

# Bringing Energy: Prophecy

We all know plants need water, but you may not know all the reasons water is needed. Water is one of the raw materials of photosynthesis. Green cells use light energy to manufacture sugars and other nutrients.[1] Without the pipes bringing the water, the plant is deprived of raw material for its essential energy production.

The spiritual gift of prophecy brings energy to people. It provides energy from the Holy Spirit to help people make connections of head, heart, and soul. When prophecy touches a dry soul, eyes open, ears hear, direction is set, and God is seen.

## What is Prophecy?

Prophecy is at best, only partially understood. In church world, prophecy is often understood to mean someone who can tell the future. It's often assumed that this insight into coming doom or deliverance refers to the second coming of Jesus. Prophecy, however, is much more than that.

---

1  Frederick S. Davies and Larry K. Jackson, <u>Citrus Growing in Florida, p. 188.</u>

In Romans 12:6, the Greek word used is *propheteian.* It's easy to see this word is the foundation of our English word "prophet." The base meaning of the word is to speak out loud the thoughts and intentions of God. Prophecy is more than delivering a message; it is understanding the message and sharing what God is saying and doing.

If this is the kind of pipe you have, you can see what God is doing; then you tell others. You can look at life's realities, read scripture, pray, and connect them. When people receive the connections, it brings energy, insight, and momentum to their lives.

Prophets might preach, but they also might offer words of counsel over a cup of coffee. Prophets might tell about the future, but they also might interpret the past. Prophets might thunder words of judgment, but they also might offer tears of sorrow. Prophets might use powerful words, but they also might use powerful actions.

Do not quickly assume that this gift is reserved for pastors. One of the Old Testament prophets, Amos, was quick to declare, "[14]I was neither a prophet nor the son of a prophet, but I was a shepherd, and I also took care of sycamore-fig trees."[2] God gave the gift of prophecy to a farmer, not professional clergy.

Prophets create vision. They see what God is doing and paint pictures, sometimes with words, sometimes with enacted parables. Listen to Isaiah describe the day of salvation:

---

2  Amos 7:14.

⁵ Then will the eyes of the blind be opened
   and the ears of the deaf unstopped.
⁶ Then will the lame leap like a deer,
   and the mute tongue shout for joy.
Water will gush forth in the wilderness
   and streams in the desert.
⁷ The burning sand will become a pool,
   the thirsty ground bubbling springs.
In the haunts where jackals once lay,
   grass and reeds and papyrus will grow.³

This is a picture of what God is going to do, vividly described.

Prophets would sometimes do odd things to describe what God was up to. Isaiah was given such an assignment:

> ¹In the year that the supreme commander, sent by Sargon king of Assyria, came to Ashdod and attacked and captured it— ² at that time the Lord spoke through Isaiah son of Amoz. He said to him, "Take off the sackcloth from your body and the sandals from your feet." And he did so, going around stripped and barefoot.

> ³Then the Lord said, "Just as my servant Isaiah has gone stripped and barefoot for three years, as a sign and portent against Egypt and Cush,"⁴ so the king of Assyria will lead away stripped and barefoot the Egyptian captives and Cushite exiles, young and old, with buttocks bared—to Egypt's shame.⁴

---

3  Isaiah 35:5-7.

4  Isaiah 20:1-4.

As one who has the gift of prophecy, let me say I pray God never gives me this assignment. But it was a conversation starter. "Isaiah, where are your clothes?" "God is going to judge Egypt and Ethiopia and they will be led away naked." "Oh, okay." The picture is painted.

What the words and actions have in common is they create a reaction. Sometimes the reaction is positive: people turn toward God. Sometimes it is negative: people stone the prophet. When the gift of prophecy is used, a spiritual energy is created either towards God or away from God.

## Biblical Examples of the Gift of Prophecy

Moses, Samuel, Elijah, Isaiah, Ezekiel, and Daniel were all considered prophets. Moses brought the teaching of God to the people who had just been delivered from slavery. Samuel plainly told the nation of Israel God didn't want them to have a king, but if they insisted, a king would be chosen. Isaiah spoke truth to power. Ezekiel helped exiles in a strange land understand what God was up to. Daniel interpreted troubling dreams and helped people understand what lay in the distant future.

Jeremiah was given the gift of prophecy, though he declared himself unworthy:

> "[6]Alas, Sovereign Lord," I said, "I do not know how to speak; I am too young."[5]

If you have the gift of prophecy, you frequently feel inadequate. It is the natural reaction to speaking for a holy and perfect God. Pride is

---

5  Jeremiah 1:6.

often a mark of a false prophet; he or she has no idea of the responsibility they hold.

Jeremiah struggled with the weight of this gift, frequently falling into depression:

15 They keep saying to me,
  "Where is the word of the Lord?
  Let it now be fulfilled!"
16 I have not run away from being your shepherd;
  you know I have not desired the day of despair.
  What passes my lips is open before you.[6]

Because prophecy often creates a negative spiritual energy, people with this gift are prone to depression. Jeremiah healthily brings his depression and anger to God. While the causes of prophetic depression vary, it often rises from a sense of speaking for God and being mocked. Frequently the reaction of people is, "Who do you think you are?"

People in Jeremiah's hometown threatened to kill him:

21 Therefore this is what the Lord says about the people of Anathoth who are threatening to kill you, saying, "Do not prophesy in the name of the Lord or you will die by our hands"— 22 therefore this is what the Lord Almighty says: "I will punish them. Their young men will die by the sword, their sons and daughters by famine.[7]

---

6  Jeremiah 17:15-16.

7  Jeremiah 11:21-22.

When God truly speaks, it is a fearful thing. Attacks come because people confuse the message with the messenger.

At this point, you may be asking if there is any upside to having this gift. For Jeremiah, the answer was a resounding "yes." God told him to buy a field in his hometown of Anathoth while Jerusalem was under siege. Imagine using scarce resources to buy a piece of property the Babylonian army was sitting on! He was to buy the field as a sign of hope, even though the city was under attack, God still had a future for his people. Jeremiah executed the transaction, and then tied the pieces of his past messages together and laced it with hope:

> [24] "See how the siege ramps are built up to take the city. Because of the sword, famine and plague, the city will be given into the hands of the Babylonians who are attacking it. What you said has happened, as you now see. [25] And though the city will be given into the hands of the Babylonians, you, Sovereign Lord, say to me, 'Buy the field with silver and have the transaction witnessed."[8]

The joy of prophecy is seeing God do exactly what he promised and reminding people there is a bigger plan in motion than the pain and heart ache of the moment.

It is falsely thought that the gift of prophecy is reserved for men. This is not so. Miriam and Deborah are referred to as prophetesses. Miriam clearly leads the women in singing God's praises in Exodus 15.

---

8   Jeremiah 32:24-25.

When Josiah was king, the Book of the Law was discovered in the Temple, apparently long neglected. He sought counsel from a woman, Huldah, who had the gift of prophecy:

> [14] Hilkiah the priest, Ahikam, Akbor, Shaphan and Asaiah went to speak to the prophet Huldah, who was the wife of Shallum son of Tikvah, the son of Harhas, keeper of the wardrobe. She lived in Jerusalem, in the New Quarter.
>
> [15] She said to them, "This is what the Lord, the God of Israel, says: Tell the man who sent you to me, [16] 'This is what the Lord says: I am going to bring disaster on this place and its people, according to everything written in the book the king of Judah has read. [17] Because they have forsaken me and burned incense to other gods and aroused my anger by all the idols their hands have made, my anger will burn against this place and will not be quenched.' [18] Tell the king of Judah, who sent you to inquire of the Lord, 'This is what the Lord, the God of Israel, says concerning the words you heard: [19] Because your heart was responsive and you humbled yourself before the Lord when you heard what I have spoken against this place and its people—that they would become a curse and be laid waste—and because you tore your robes and wept in my presence, I also have heard you, declares the Lord. [20] Therefore I will gather you to your ancestors, and you will be buried in peace. Your eyes will not see all the disaster I am going to bring on this place.'"
>
> So they took her answer back to the king.[9]

---

9  2 Kings 22:14-20.

This is an amazing picture! The King wants to inquire of the Lord. So a priest, the King's secretary, and two other men make their way to a woman, who confidently speaks God's word to them, to relay to the King. Her word contains a prediction of the future ("my anger will burn against this place"), words of grace ("you will be buried in peace"), and a pronouncement of judgment ("your eyes will not see all the disaster I am going to bring"). This is not preaching; these are words of wisdom offered to a small audience.

Huldah's words energized Josiah in a positive direction, as the gift of prophecy is designed to do:

> [3] The king stood by the pillar and renewed the covenant in the presence of the Lord—to follow the Lord and keep his commands, statutes and decrees with all his heart and all his soul, thus confirming the words of the covenant written in this book. Then all the people pledged themselves to the covenant.[10]

Jeremiah and Huldah (who lived in the same time) are examples of how the gift of prophecy brings energy to people by bringing insight into the ways of God.

## Ways the gift of Prophecy is used

The gift of prophecy is in use whenever a legitimate insight about God is brought to another person. The gift is connected with language, spoken or written.

When we interpret and apply scripture to real life, we are exercising prophecy. I was at a low point in my life and spoke to a counselor

---

10  2 Kings 23:3.

friend of mine. After hearing my troubles, he pulled out his Bible, and shared these words:

> ² Praise the Lord, my soul,
>    and forget not all his benefits—
> ³ who forgives all your sins
>    and heals all your diseases,
> ⁴ who redeems your life from the pit
>    and crowns you with love and compassion,
> ⁵ who satisfies your desires with good things
>    so that your youth is renewed like the eagle's.[11]

My counselor friend prophesied to me. He applied the right passage at the right time to the wounded place of my soul.

Spiritual directors often use this gift. They are skilled at bringing God's message to someone who needs to face a challenge. John Ortberg was going through a difficult period in his life. He shared his struggles with his mentor Dallas Willard, who told him, "You must ruthlessly eliminate hurry from your life." That's prophecy!

Prophets proclaim messages from God. This happens when someone speaks to a group on behalf of God. This expression of prophesy is preaching. Not all preaching is prophecy. Some sermons are compilations of clever outlines and good jokes. True prophetic preaching is bringing a message from God that applies to a group or to an individual in such a way that energy is created.

---

11   Psalm 103:2-5.

When a preacher calls a church to action to care for the poor, that is prophesy. When a sermon is delivered that encourages individuals to give, that is prophesy. When a message is brought that explains the process of God's sanctifying work, that is prophecy.

When a leader of God's people calls them to take an amazing journey (like Moses), that's prophecy. Creating vision for what can be when God's leadership is followed is prophecy creating energy.

Prophecy can be predictive. This is not as mysterious as it sounds. Scripture provides basic guidance. God will judge sins of individuals and nations. God honors repentance. God celebrates when people come to Him. When the timeline and the players get specific, one must be careful. To speak for God falsely is to be a "false" prophet.

Some people claim to have this gift, but in fact lead people astray. In Deuteronomy 13, this specific warning is given:

> [1]If a prophet, or one who foretells by dreams, appears among you and announces to you a sign or wonder, [2] and if the sign or wonder spoken of takes place, and the prophet says, "Let us follow other gods" (gods you have not known) "and let us worship them," [3] you must not listen to the words of that prophet or dreamer. The Lord your God is testing you to find out whether you love him with all your heart and with all your soul. [4] It is the Lord your God you must follow, and him you must revere. Keep his commands and obey him; serve him and hold fast to him.[12]

---

12  Deuteronomy 13:1-4.

A false prophet is one who leads away from God. Whenever someone distorts the teaching of God, when a person adds to or takes away from scripture, they are trying to be a prophet, but they are not exercising the gift of prophecy.

Prophecy is not restricted to the spoken word. In my opinion, the best worship leaders have this gift. They are able to bring a congregation into the presence of God and help them all see what God is doing. Worship leaders with this gift are able to be the pipe which ushers people into God's presence.

## You might have the gift of prophecy if:

- You are able to speak for God in an energizing way.
- You can speak, sing or pray in front of people.
- People come to you for guidance or advice.
- You hear whispers from God that align with His word.
- When people follow your counsel, God blesses them.
- You are able to see a picture of the future that conforms to God's desires.
- You feel closest to God when you are speaking for God.

## What to do if you have this gift

If you have the gift of prophecy, immerse yourself in the study of God's word. The sharpness of your gift is enhanced by your knowledge of God's word. The best pattern of study is to read the Bible through each year. Repeated exposure will allow you to absorb large themes of scripture. Most false prophecy occurs when a person blows a single verse out of proportion. Frank Tupper, my theology professor in seminary, said that most heresies start with a misinterpretation of John 1:1.

Match your study of God's word with a deep prayer life. Develop the skill of listening in prayer. Invite God to speak to you. Ask God to open your eyes to what he is doing in the world. It is essential that you pray before you speak for God. The prayer might be just a phrase, but you want to be connected to God when you speak for God.

Both of these disciplines mold your spirit so you are thinking as God thinks (as best a human can do) and are speaking words that God would speak.

If you think you have this gift, try it out. Although I did not realize it at the time, my first use of the prophetic gift was in middle school. I was sitting on the bleachers with some friends, and one friend, Karl, began to talk about questions he had about God. Though I was in seventh grade, I was able to answer Karl's questions in a helpful way. I still remember as I was speaking to him thinking, "I don't know where these answers are coming from. I'm not that smart." I wasn't but God is! Karl, who is still a friend, tells me he still remembers that conversation. I think he remembers because the conversation wasn't from me, but from God.

If the gift of prophecy is matched with a comfort of being in front of people, seek an opportunity to speak or preach. Measure people's response – if energy comes, you are prophesying.

Again, having the gift of prophecy does not mean you are automatically called to vocational ministry. My cousin Marcus has the gift, yet he is a cattleman. Marcus speaks at most of the funerals in our hometown and often fills in for the pastor of his church when he is gone.

His words bring a comforting energy to people. Marcus isn't a clergy person; but he has the gift and uses it for God.

As this gift grows, begin each day with a prayer that you will be aware of people that God brings to you. Listen for opportunities to share who God is and what He is doing. Prophecy is an attractional gift. People will be drawn to you because you will be able to bring the wisdom and energy they need for life.

The temptation for people with this gift is to forget they are the pipe. They begin to believe they are the water that brings energy. Never lose sight that you are the pipe!

If you have the gift of prophecy, you must match it with courage. Prophecy can create negative energy. It takes courage to speak for God to a group that is hostile. It takes courage to paint a vision for a church or a group of God's people that challenges status quo. Courage is required to take the plunge into a conversation and take it to a deeper level. Ask God to grow your courage!

## What this gift looks like in real life

My teacher Henlee Barnette had this gift. He courageously stood against racial segregation and inequality in the 1950's and 1960. His prophetic gift was expressed in the classroom, challenging the views of racist students from the Deep South. He opened the door for Martin Luther King, Jr. to come to The Southern Baptist Theological Seminary to speak, a courageous act in those days. Duke McCall, president of the Seminary at the time, estimated King's visit cost the seminary $400,000 in gifts that were withdrawn. Dr. Barnette knew God's truth needed to be shared, no matter the price.

My friend David has the gift of prophecy. While David was a pastor, now he is a chemistry professor. David comes from a Pentecostal background and has an open spirit to hear from God. Occasionally, David will stop by my office, and ask how I am doing. I will share whatever is going on, and then David will think for a moment, and then share what God is impressing on him.

One day, David came by, and I was sharing with him some particularly tough decisions I needed to make and some personal transitions. David thought for a moment and said to me, "I feel impressed to tell you that you are the presence of the Father's heart."

Those prophetic words knocked me over. God sent a message through them: no matter the stress I felt, I was to remember that I was a pipe. What mattered was the Father's heart and how I could bring it to people. My friend David prophesied to me that day.

Prophets bring the life giving water that energizes the tree – and fruit grows.

### Where from here

If you think you have the gift of prophecy, be open to God. Speak for him when the doors open. Immerse yourself in his word. Be the pipe that brings energy.

# CHAPTER 3

# Getting Water
# Where it Needs to Go:
# Service

Pipes serve. They have no value just sitting in a stack. When pipes are stored, they aren't fulfilling their purpose. But when pipes connect, they serve both the well and the tree. They serve the well by taking the life-giving water and directing it where it is needed. They serve the tree by bringing the tree exactly what it needs. The water has to move from source to need. When a pipe does this, it performs the gift of service.

## The Biblical Definition of Service

Romans 12:7 continues the thought of Romans 12:6:

> [6]If your gift is prophesying, then prophesy in accordance with your faith; [7] if it is serving, then serve.

Biblical Greek uses several different words to describe servants and service. In general, Greeks thought serving was not dignified. The goal in Greek life was to be served, not to serve. Judaism brought to the world the idea that loving your neighbor as yourself was something noble and good.[1] The Jesus movement expanded this concept by connecting service with love.

One Greek word for service is *diakonian*, which means to serve or to take care of someone. Paul uses this word here. It is often connected with serving someone a meal; in essence, to be a waiter or a waitress.[2] Jesus declared himself to be this kind of servant during the Last Supper. Catching yet another whiff of the old argument of who was the greatest disciple, Jesus said:

> [27]For who is greater, the one who is at the table or the one who serves? Is it not the one who is at the table? But I am among you as one who serves.[3]

Jesus' reason for service was not for his gain; he serves because he loves. His service is a gift of grace. You know you have this gift when serving is an act of love, not a chore or a duty.

*Diakonian* is used in the New Testament to describe specific people, such as Timothy.[4] It can also refer to someone who serves a spiritual power, whether the power is good or evil.[5] Unbelieving government authorities are also called servants of God because they maintain

---

1  Leviticus 19:18.

2  Theological Dictionary of the New Testament, vol. II, pp. 81-87.

3  Luke 22:27.

4  1 Thessalonians 3:1-3.

5  For example, 2 Corinthians 11:14.

God's order in the world.[6] It is also the basis for the word "deacon," used to refer to servants of the church.[7]

The specific idea conveyed by *diakonian* is service given, not demanded. The motivation of service is not fear, but love. The true servant answers to his or her master because of affection for the master. Directions are received because the servant is loyal to the cause of the master.

The gift of service is the most common gift. This is perhaps because the need for this gift to be used for Jesus is so great. All followers of Jesus are to serve him:

Whoever serves me must follow me; and where I am, my servant also will be. My Father will honor the one who serves me.[8]

If this is not your natural inclination, it is an indication you need the Holy Spirit to grow a more attentive, empathetic, giving heart. If serving is a natural tendency, then you will find yourself enjoying opportunities to help others, especially by doing something for them.

## Biblical Examples of Service

All the great figures of the Bible – Noah, Abraham, Moses, Joshua, David, Peter, and Paul were servants of God. They did not all have the gift of service. They used their gifts, whatever they were, to serve God. They applied their gifts to the call God put on their lives.

In Acts 6, the disciples rightly understand their gifts call them to serve the word of God. They invite the church to choose seven men full of

---

6   Revelation 13:1-4.

7   1 Timothy 3:8-13.

8   John 12:26.

the Spirit and wisdom to serve the widows of the church. The church through the centuries recognizes these men as servants/deacons.

Why was it important to have men full of the Spirit and wisdom? The Spirit would energize these men toward service. This is a hallmark of the service gift. Those who have it move toward those in need. They are not compelled to service; they long to serve. Wisdom is required to understand the true need. Often the presenting need is not the real need. For example, a family may need food. Someone with the gift of service will provide them food. When service is guided by wisdom, the server asks, "Why is this family without food? Is there a medical need that prohibits work? Are they ignorant of job opportunities? Is the Mom or Dad lazy?" Wisdom makes sure service helps, not hurts.

Of the seven men chosen, we know the most about Stephen and Philip. Stephen served by deploying additional gifts of wonders and signs (miracles). He spoke with great wisdom and was finally stoned because of his bold witness.[9] Philip is forced to leave Jerusalem when persecution arises. He proclaims the good news of Jesus, performing signs and healings. Philip is guided by the Spirit away from Samaria to a desolate stretch of road, where he is drawn to the Ethiopian eunuch. Seeing and hearing him read Isaiah, Philip moves toward him, helps him find Jesus, and baptizes him.

Both of these men use their gifts of service to enhance their other gift of prophecy. You may have the gift of prophecy or teaching that is accelerated by your gift of service.

---

9  In my opinion, signs and wonders fall under the broad category of the prophetic gift, because the purpose of a sign or a wonder is to point to God.

In Romans 16, Paul tells us of an extraordinary servant of God:

> [1] I commend to you our sister Phoebe, a deacon (servant) of the church in Cenchreae. [2] I ask you to receive her in the Lord in a way worthy of his people and to give her any help she may need from you, for she has been the benefactor of many people, including me.[10]

Theologians and preachers debate back and forth whether Phoebe held the office of deacon. Clearly she had the gift of service. So put aside the question of women serving as deacons. What kind of servant was she?

Phoebe served the church. The gift of service is to be deployed for the body of Christ. This means the church must help people with the gift of service find ways and places of service! It also means Phoebe didn't free-lance. There are many opportunities to serve outside the church. Those with the true spiritual gift of service feel drawn to serve the Jesus movement in a specific place. In Phoebe's case, it was the church at Cenchreae.

Cenchreae was a village near Corinth. It was a port village, bustling with trade. The Corinth area was a morally challenging area. In Paul's letters to the Corinthians, he must tell them not to sue each other; to adhere to sexual boundaries; to respect all persons, rich and poor, the same; and to have a humble attitude about their spiritual gifting. In this environment, Phoebe serves Jesus' church.

---

10   Romans 16:1-2

Phoebe is described as a benefactor of many people. The Greek word means to be a patroness, a provider, or a helper. Phoebe invested not only her time, but her resources as well. This is the mark of someone with the gift of service: they invest all of who they are in helping.

Often sin can enter the life of someone with the gift of service. They believe they give their time and skill by helping; therefore, they do not have to give their money. This is a clear sign that pride has inhabited their hearts and is inhibiting their gift of service. Having one gift does not exempt you from doing what Jesus commands.

Phoebe is apparently on her way to Rome. Paul instructs believers there to receive her and give her help. She would need to be encouraged by fellow followers of Jesus and she would need assistance in her helping.

This reiterates the role of God's people toward those who have the gift of service. They need a strong family of faith to support them. They need to be helped so they can help. The kind of help Phoebe is to receive is not specified. It may have been financial assistance, or helping her orient to a new city. Paul might have known she would need to be connected to certain kinds of people for her particular gift to be used. This is what the church is to do: create an environment where people with the gift of service can serve and help!

## How to use the gift of Service

Jesus told us how to use the gift of service:

> "31When the Son of Man comes in his glory, and all the angels with him, he will sit on his glorious throne. 32 All the nations will be gathered before him, and he will separate the people one

from another as a shepherd separates the sheep from the goats. [33] He will put the sheep on his right and the goats on his left.

[34] "Then the King will say to those on his right, 'Come, you who are blessed by my Father; take your inheritance, the kingdom prepared for you since the creation of the world. [35] For I was hungry and you gave me something to eat, I was thirsty and you gave me something to drink, I was a stranger and you invited me in, [36] I needed clothes and you clothed me, I was sick and you looked after me, I was in prison and you came to visit me.'

[37] "Then the righteous will answer him, 'Lord, when did we see you hungry and feed you, or thirsty and give you something to drink? [38] When did we see you a stranger and invite you in, or needing clothes and clothe you? [39] When did we see you sick or in prison and go to visit you?'

[40] "The King will reply, 'Truly I tell you, whatever you did for one of the least of these brothers and sisters of mine, you did for me.'

[41] "Then he will say to those on his left, 'Depart from me, you who are cursed, into the eternal fire prepared for the devil and his angels. [42] For I was hungry and you gave me nothing to eat, I was thirsty and you gave me nothing to drink, [43] I was a stranger and you did not invite me in, I needed clothes and you did not clothe me, I was sick and in prison and you did not look after me.'

[44] "They also will answer, 'Lord, when did we see you hungry or thirsty or a stranger or needing clothes or sick or in prison, and did not help you?'

[45] "He will reply, 'Truly I tell you, whatever you did not do for one of the least of these, you did not do for me.'

[46] "Then they will go away to eternal punishment, but the righteous to eternal life."[11]

People who have the gift of service see a person in need, and they see Jesus. They see each person is loved by God. They know God wants to bring grace and hope. They see themselves as the ones to bring what God wants.

Gifts of service are most often deployed in the face of physical need. Servers want to provide for those who cannot provide for themselves. They work in food banks and soup kitchens, seeing in every hungry face the face of Jesus. Servers respond when disaster strikes to make sure there is clean water to drink. They go and drill wells in remote places in the world so water borne diseases do not spread.

People with the gift of service are hospitable. They make others feel at home. Service expressed as hospitality can mean taking in children no one else wants; it can mean hosting a Biblical study in your home; it can mean bringing meals to those grieving or recovering from illness. Service with hospitality can be used within the body to make sure first time attenders feel welcomed and loved.

---

11   Matthew 25:31-46.

People with the gift of service and mercy excel at the ministry of being with people. They know how to visit in hospitals, nursing homes, and assisted living facilities. They recognize Jesus' most important work may be to hold the hand of someone who is sick.

Servers go to people who cannot come for help. They visit in prisons and jails. They believe everyone deserves God's grace.

Great work is done in Jesus' name when gifts of service are deployed. Hospitals and orphanages rise around the world. Prisons are transformed from places of darkness to places of light. Wheelchair ramps are built, babies are rocked, furniture is moved, laundry is done, meals are cooked, and houses are cleaned. Churches vibrate with authenticity because people see, not just sense, care.

When people with the gift of service act, non-believers take notice. Non-believers may not agree with our teaching or believe in our God, but they appreciate service. The gift of service gives the Jesus movement credibility. In the early days of the Jesus movement, it was the followers of Jesus caring for people everyone else abandoned that gained them the most credibility.

Many new paradigm churches no longer have people serving as "Deacons." I think this is a mistake. While in the past many churches had a "Board of Deacons," this was never the intention of the early church. Deacons were selected to serve Jesus' church, to do whatever needed to be done.

At the church I serve, our Deacons focus on five areas:

- Visiting everyone in our local hospital every day of the year.
- Reaching out to first time guests by bringing them a gift.
- Serving a meal to those interested in joining the church family.
- Being proactive resolvers of conflict.
- Giving wisdom about the church's direction and future from a servant's perspective.

What church wouldn't want a group to serve the church and do these things?

## You might have this gift if:

- You like to help others.
- You like to do more than talk.
- You like to do projects or tasks.
- You have a heart for the disadvantaged.
- If you see someone who needs help, you stop and offer help.
- You have trouble saying "no" to people who need assistance.
- You notice people on the fringe.
- You would rather be behind the scenes than up in front of people.
- Your heart has the spirit of "yes" instead of "no."
- You volunteer for projects.

## Putting this gift to work

Chances are if you have the gift of service, you are already using it! You move toward people in need. Usually God places in the heart of one who serves a calling to certain kinds of need or hurt. For example, one person with the gift of service is drawn to serve children; another is drawn to serve people in jail. The gift is matched with a calling.

To discover if you have this gift, do a "First Serve." A "First Serve" is stepping into a ministry area where you feel called. Do you find yourself moving toward those being served?

Our church regularly joins with other churches in the area to feed the men and women who work at the annual county fair. These folks often live in travel trailers and exist on fair food (delicious, but not nutritious). The times I have attended this event, I can easily tell who has the gift of service. Those who have the gift of service but lack the gift of mercy are in the kitchen, happily preparing some home cooking for the fair workers. Those who have the service gift and the gift of mercy are talking to the fair workers. Those who do not have the gift of service are checking their phones for messages.

The best check to see if you have this gift is to pay attention to yourself. Do you move toward filling a need? When you fill the need, are people blessed?

As you grow this gift, find a way to serve regularly. Discover your particular calling. Incorporate serving into your schedule. In our busy world, if we wait until the right moment to serve, we will miss growing our gift.

As you begin to serve regularly, be self-aware and discover if you are a marathoner or a sprinter. Marathoners cover a long distance over a long period of time. Sprinters focus energy into short bursts to cover short distances as fast as possible.

Servers who are marathoners excel at always being there. If an act of service needs to be done, daily or weekly, a marathon server is your person. Servers who are sprinters are great in crisis or for projects. A sprinter server loves cleaning an elderly person's home on a special church service day or being on a crisis response team for disasters. One way is not better than the other; both are needed. Marathoners get frustrated if assigned repeated sprinter tasks because they feel like they never get in a groove. Sprinters get frustrated with marathon needs because the joy of the finish line doesn't come very often.

Whether you are a marathoner or a sprinter, regular service is essential to growing your gift.

Ultimately those with the gift of service want to embrace the life of service. People with a life of service begin to see needs as God sees them. They find themselves meeting needs they did not even know existed. They will find new skills rising, so they can meet new needs. People who live a life of service often are admired with puzzlement. Few understand how such joy can come from meeting the needs of others.

All gifts carry danger. The danger of the gift of service is that you will burn out. This happens because your calling to serve will blind you to your need to rest. I've seen people become exhausted and bitter ("Why isn't anyone else coming to help me help?") because they ignored the commandment to labor six days and rest on the seventh. Servers sometimes forgo vacation because they can't imagine anyone taking their place. Thus service can lead to an odd spiritual pride of indispensability. Servers need rest; they need a break. They need to be fed.

I've also seen servers hide from God by serving. In one church I pastored, an older lady kept preschool children during the worship service for years. We all admired her faithfulness. It was not until her sudden death that I discovered she was estranged from her sister and one of her sons. She held onto great bitterness and didn't want to hear songs and messages about forgiveness.

A common frustration for a team of servers is leadership. Typically a group of servers gather to do a project. One of the servers is selected as the leader. This is a frustrating position for some servers, because they want to be doing, not leading. As a result, the team is poorly led, frustrations arise, and the one appointed leader feels in over his or her head. There is a simple solution: every team of servants needs a leader who helps them serve. The leader organizes and sets the win; the servers do the mission.

If you have the gift of service with the gift of leadership, you are leading from a position of care. The gift of service and leadership combined is the best definition of a servant leader.

## What this gift looks like in real life

Jo had the gift of service. When I first came to pastor Alice Drive, Miss Jo came by our house on her grandson's four-wheeler, offering to help us unpack. That was the first of many gracious, serving acts on her part. Jo worked in Children's Ministry each Sunday, she served in the kitchen, and she was faithful to go with me each Monday to visit first time guests to our church.

I learned that Jo's gift of service was a truly a life of service. Whenever our family would have a garage sale, Jo would come and help us organize, price, and sell. Her prices were always low – because she knew we were selling clothes to people who didn't have deep pockets; she wanted to serve them. I know Jo would go over to her friend's homes to help them clean out closets and attics. Wherever she saw the need, she filled it.

Another great servant at Alice Drive was Forist. Forist served our country as a pilot and an engineer. Then he served the military by helping people invest for their future. But Forist's service was not limited to his work life.

He taught an adult group; he sang in the choir (even after he had hearing aids); he served as a Deacon. But more than this, Forist taught immigrants how to drive; he did taxes for widows; he did laundry for a paraplegic; he took a mental disturbed woman to the hospital (over and over). When I casually mentioned I didn't know how I would fix the sprinkler system manifold in my yard, he came over (without my knowledge) and fixed it. It remains to this day the best engineered sprinkler manifold in our city. When Forist saw the need, he moved to meet the need as best he could.

Miss Jo and Forist lived servants' lives, deploying their gifts in a way that brought honor to God.

### Where from here

If you read this chapter and felt your mind drift toward a need you know exists, you probably have the gift of service. Go serve. If at first you get no response, keep knocking. Don't wait for permission! Dive in. You are the pipe that connects the grace of Jesus with people who need to know that grace is real.

# CHAPTER 4

# Encouraging Root Growth: Teaching

My family still owns the orange groves of my childhood, but the way the trees are irrigated has changed. Now instead of moving aluminum pipes around, plastic pipe runs down every row. Inserted into the plastic pipe under each tree is a small plastic tube, topped by a miniature sprinkler called a micro-jet. This method of irrigation puts the water right where it needs to be, close to the tree's roots.

Over time, the tree grows more roots in the wet zone created by the micro-jet. You can see why. In dry times, when the tree is under stress, the roots in the wet zone get the moisture. The larger the wet zone, the healthier the tree.

The gift of teaching is like a micro-jet. It creates a "nourishment zone" where the life-giving water of Jesus can be absorbed by dry lives. The stronger the gift of teaching is, the larger the nourishment zone is.

The gift of teaching is the pipe that helps lives grow strong roots.

## What is teaching?

In Romans 12:7, Paul continues his thoughts about using spiritual gifts in accordance with your faith. He says:

> if it is teaching, then teach…

The Greek word translated here as "teaching" is *Didaschon*. It means to instruct or to impart information. It holds in tension two aspects of teaching: the knowledge presupposed in the teacher and the arrival of insight to the one who is being taught.[1] To hold knowledge and to speak it is not true teaching. To present knowledge in such a way that another receives it and is changed by that knowledge is to have the gift of teaching. Teaching builds a bridge.

The temptation is to see the gift of teaching only in a school or university setting. This was not the model of Biblical times. In Jesus' day, people would seek instruction from a person, not an institution. Teachers, also called "Rabbis," were people who interpreted the scripture to a group of people. People in the groups were called "disciples," from the Greek word meaning "apprentice." The disciples would spend time with the teacher, doing life with him, asking questions, probing for deeper understanding of God and His word. Teaching was strongly connected to Scripture, with particular focus on the first five books of the Old Testament.

The first five books of the Old Testament were (and are still by Jews) called the *Torah*. *Torah* in Hebrew is often translated as "law." The word is broader than this single definition, however. *Torah* also means

---

1  Theological Dictionary of the New Testament, Vol. II, p. 135.

"teaching," "instruction," and "revelation." Thus in Jesus' day, teachers taught the teaching.

This Biblical pattern opens our understanding to the gift of teaching. When imparted from the Holy Spirit, it is a gift that allows one to learn the scripture and then convey the meaning of the scripture to a group of people who are in a particular place and time.

Exercising this gift looks less like a lecture and more like a coach directing a team. It is essential that all have the same understanding of the plays being called and goals being sought. A good coach gives knowledge and helps his players apply it to a game. Someone with the gift of teaching explains the Word of God and helps people apply it to real life – and then he or she sees them do it!

## Biblical Examples of the Gift of Teaching

Solomon, King of Israel, had this gift. Most of his teaching is recorded in Proverbs. As the book opens, he states his purpose:

> ¹The proverbs of Solomon son of David, king of Israel:
>
> ² for gaining wisdom and instruction;
>    for understanding words of insight;
> ³ for receiving instruction in prudent behavior,
>    doing what is right and just and fair;
> ⁴ for giving prudence to those who are simple,
>    knowledge and discretion to the young—
> ⁵ let the wise listen and add to their learning,
>    and let the discerning get guidance—

[6] for understanding proverbs and parables,
   the sayings and riddles of the wise.[2]

Solomon says his purpose is to help people gain wisdom. Wisdom is a key component of the gift of teaching. Wisdom is the ability not only to have knowledge, but to rightly apply that knowledge. Wisdom recognizes while every scripture is inspired, not every scripture applies to every situation.

Solomon offers his teaching to the simple, or we might say, "the gullible." These are people who have no filters to understand what they are hearing. But Solomon's teaching is also for the wise. Wise people know they never know enough; they are perpetual learners. Those who develop the gift of teaching are able, with the same instruction, to reach both the beginner and the expert.

The teaching of Proverbs is found in poems, pithy sayings, and stories. A teacher places material into a form that engages the mind. Nowhere are Jesus' followers encouraged to memorize dry facts; instead, scripture comes in forms that make us think.

In John 13:13, Jesus acknowledged that the disciples called Him "teacher" and said they were correct, because that's what He was. Jesus, being our ultimate teacher, also taught in a way that engaged people. He spoke with authority built on knowledge:

---

2  Proverbs 1:1-6.

[28] When Jesus had finished saying these things, the crowds were amazed at his teaching, [29] because he taught as one who had authority, and not as their teachers of the law.[3]

Like Solomon, Jesus used parables, stories with a sharp point. More than once, his disciples approached him and asked Him to explain a parable because they did not understand. This, of course, did not reflect on Jesus ineffectiveness as a teacher. Rather, the disciples' lack of understanding reveals the teacher's greatest frustration. A teacher may explain everything perfectly and yet the students are not yet able or willing (or both) to accept the wisdom offered.

While Paul does not refer to himself as a teacher, he is described as one by Luke:

> [11]So Paul stayed in Corinth for a year and a half, teaching them the word of God.[4]

Paul probably did not refer to himself as a teacher because he wanted no confusion about the Jesus movement, so the movement looked to Jesus alone as teacher. But Paul did all the work of a teacher. While he made tents in Corinth, he taught people about Jesus. He explained how the Scriptures (in Paul's day, the Old Testament) spoke of Jesus. He wrote letters to Jesus followers as a way to pass on his knowledge of God and His Word.

His teaching resulted in life change – and still does! He would write to churches, and they would change their actions. Preachers and teachers

---

3   Matthew 7:28-29.

4   Acts 18:11.

today speak from those same words, and churches today change directions. Paul would share knowledge, and people would see that following Jesus made sense. People read Paul's words today, and they still think it makes sense to follow Jesus. The gift of teaching can have eternal impact.

## Ways the gift of Teaching is used

There is a distinction between those who have aptitude for teaching and those who have the spiritual gift of teaching. Someone with an aptitude for teaching might be effective as a school teacher, or a football coach, or a professor. To hold the spiritual gift of teaching, however, means you are able to convey the truth of God – an awesome responsibility! A person may have both an aptitude for teaching and the gift of teaching, but it is not necessary to have both.

All teaching done within the context of spiritual giftedness is rooted in God's teaching. This requires understanding God's teaching and the study of Scripture. One with the gift of teaching is always asking, "Does what I teach conform to God's word?" Thus, one with the teaching gift must also be a learner. They must learn not just the Bible, but how the Bible conveys truth. The words of Scripture are important, but so are the forms that hold the words. Someone with the gift of teaching is hungry to learn about ancient backgrounds so a passage of Scripture can be properly understood.

If you have the gift of teaching, you want to share it with someone whose life could change because of what you share. You may impart this knowledge to a group of people, or to two or three people, or to one person.

People with the gift of teaching often find themselves drawn to teach a group because they enjoy what they learn in preparing to lead the group.

The gift of teaching, as mentioned above, is akin to coaching. In our time, coaching is not limited to the ball field. CEOs and organizations engage coaches (sometimes called "consultants") to help them overcome a barrier in performance. The same is true of those with the spiritual gift of teaching. A teacher may function more as a coach, giving one on one attention to someone, or helping them with a particular skill.

A new follower of Jesus, I'll call Mary, made an appointment to see me about her prayer life. She had unfortunately been taught falsely that prayer was like placing an online order. Once she made the request, she assumed the answer would show up in a few days. I was able to teach her, one on one, that prayer is not a matter of ask and receive; prayer is conversation with God. The best way to have the conversation is to be honest and ask. Then pause and listen to His response. We may find out we are asking for the wrong thing, or we may be asking at the wrong time, or we may need to trust God with an answer we cannot yet know.

Often people with the teaching gift are invited to enter a mentoring relationship with someone. This mentoring is more than encouragement; it is being transparent about how you are living out Scripture in your life. Mentoring is an intimate expression of the teaching gift.

Those with the gift of teaching are often called to share their wisdom through the written word. Some of the most influential teachers I've ever had, I've never met personally. Several, in fact, are dead. Their teaching, however, lives on, and helps me understand God's word and actions.

Just as churches open up opportunities for those with the gifts of service, churches also open up opportunities for those with the gift of teaching. The most common expression is offering teachers a chance to lead a group. Care must be given, however, so it is understood that the one with the gift of teaching may not be the best leader of the group. The group may need a separate leader in addition to its teacher.

Some churches establish mentoring programs. These can be done where older men or women mentor those younger according to the model described in Titus 2:1-8. Mentor ministries also can offer the help of older couples to younger couples.

### You might have the gift of Teaching if:

- You like to learn about the Bible.
- You like to share your learning.
- When you share what you've learned, people learn and change.
- People come to you asking questions about the Bible.
- You enjoy writing as a way to express what you've learned.
- You enjoy seeing "the lights go on" when you teach.
- You enjoy translating scripture from its original language to a modern equivalent.
- You listen to someone else teach or preach and think "I would have said that differently."

## What to do if you have this gift

Chances are if you have this gift, you have already felt drawn toward the Bible. You find at least parts of it fascinating. You probably already have a hunger to teach someone.

God blessed me with this gift. When I was eight, I was given a Good News For Modern Man New Testament. It was a paraphrase I could understand and I devoured it. Before a year passed, I had read the New Testament through four or five times. I would relish the days when our Sunday School teacher failed to show up; I would volunteer to teach the class. Immodestly, I thought I held my classmates attention better than our teacher who read out of the quarterly. I did not yet realize my hunger to read the Bible and to teach were marks of having a spiritual gift. That realization would come later.

The gift of teaching requires learning. Immerse yourself in Scripture. Make it a discipline to read the Bible through regularly; this will help you stay balanced in your understanding of the Bible. Learn about Biblical backgrounds. Invest in a good study Bible and a good Bible dictionary to help understand.

If God calls you to apply this gift in a vocational way, get all the education you can. There is an errant understanding that if you have the gift of teaching you need no school to help you. Nowhere does the Bible bless ignorance. My Uncle Dow finished his formal education with the 8th grade. After he was a man with a family, God called him to deploy his gift of teaching as a pastor of small country churches. Uncle Dow was old when I knew him, but I remember him saying to me, "I wish I could have gotten more education. There is so much in this book (meaning the Bible) I still don't know. Son, you get all you can." That's exactly what someone with the gift of teaching would say; they know teaching is given richly by learning deeply.

If you have this gift, seek opportunities to speak or write. You may want to start in a simple way: lead a short-term group at church with a video teaching curriculum. If you find during the discussion period your comments add clarity, chances are good you are uncovering your true spiritual gift.

As you use this gift, see if people are blessed. Do people thank you for helping them understand something they had not understood before? Does your life change through your preparation? Do people's lives change because of what you teach?

As your teaching gift matures, see if there is an opportunity to teach a long term group. If you don't have the gift of leadership, make sure you are not put into the class on your own! Ask for a leader to be put in a group with you.

People who teach a long term group are able to see progress in the lives of group members. Much of the progress will be measured anecdotally. People will share stories of how sharing in a group guided them in some life situation during the week. That's a sign that you have this gift.

When the gift of teaching is properly applied, others blossom and are also stirred to teach. At our church, one of our leaders, Norman, excels both at teaching and opening the door for other teachers. His group is now producing teachers for other groups. This happens because the true spiritual gift of teaching does not seek to "hog" the spotlight, but draw others into the joy of teaching.

Grow your gift of teaching by asking someone with the gift of teaching to give you suggestions for improvement. I know several folks who regularly sit down with someone in their teaching sphere and ask for help in getting better. A true teacher wants to learn to be better. I also know some with the teaching gift who are ineffective because they have never asked for help in growing their gift.

The number one mistake of people with the teaching gift is to think they are imparting knowledge. The gift of teaching is applying Scriptural truth to a particular culture in a relevant way. For example, if you have the gift of teaching and a calling to work with children, you wouldn't want to rely on teaching aids and techniques from the 1950's? A flannel-graph (a kind of Velcro board you stick pictures to) was cool in 1955; today, it's outdated. Instead, show your children a short video clip on your iPad.

If you have the gift of teaching and work with adults, remember adults learn on a need to know basis. There may be a few folks who want to learn the facts of scripture for the sake of knowledge; most other adults will be asking, "How does this impact me?" A wise teacher of adults may begin with a story that everyone can relate to, one that draws everyone in. Then they apply the scripture to the story. Or they may start with a question that is deliberately combative (for example, "How should we love Muslims?"). Then after creating tension, a spiritually gifted teacher brings the scripture to the tension: [44]"But I say to you, love your enemies; do good to those who persecute you."[5]

To be a mentor or a coach and be culturally relevant means speaking to people in real world language, not church language. For example, if

---

5  Matthew 5:44.

53

I am mentoring someone and I need to teach them about stewardship I might not start with that word. Stewardship is a church word that isn't regularly used in culture. Instead, I might talk about resource management. Most people in our culture have an instant idea of what that means.

There is a frustration in having the teaching gift. Spirit empowered teachers build bridges between themselves and people who need to learn. But the teachers cannot control the people on the other side of the bridge. Jesus told a story about this:

> [3] Then he told them many things in parables, saying: "A farmer went out to sow his seed. [4] As he was scattering the seed, some fell along the path, and the birds came and ate it up. [5] Some fell on rocky places, where it did not have much soil. It sprang up quickly, because the soil was shallow. [6] But when the sun came up, the plants were scorched, and they withered because they had no root. [7] Other seed fell among thorns, which grew up and choked the plants. [8] Still other seed fell on good soil, where it produced a crop—a hundred, sixty or thirty times what was sown. [9] Whoever has ears, let them hear."[6]

The teacher is like the sower. He scatters his knowledge and some of it never enters the life of someone who needs it. Sometimes the knowledge is received, but like seed on rocky ground, it never takes root because the receiver never reflected on it. A teacher scatters wisdom, and it is received for a moment, but it is soon choked out by other cares. But there are golden moments when the connection is made and the

---

6  Matthew 13:3-9.

one needing the knowledge is hit at just the right moment and life is changed.

The old folk saying, "When the student is ready, the teacher appears" can be modified to, "When the student is ready, God provides the teacher." This is common in my life. I face a crisis, and then I read or hear God's truth and the message fits perfectly. People will say to me, "You were preaching right to me." I smile because I know what is really happening; God has provided the right words at the right time through me.

There is a heavy responsibility with this gift. A person with the spiritual gift of teaching must live what they teach! Thousands of teachers through the centuries have tried to teach God's truth but live the devil's lie. The proof of an authentic spiritual gift properly used is found in the teacher's life. James 3 warns us:

> [1]Not many of you should become teachers, my fellow believers, because you know that we who teach will be judged more strictly.[7]

Why would a teacher be judged more strictly? One answer is they have the ability to teach something that will lead others astray. But James has something more in mind than this. He goes on to say:

> [13] Who is wise and understanding among you? Let them show it by their good life, by deeds done in the humility that comes from wisdom. [14] But if you harbor bitter envy and selfish ambition in your hearts, do not boast about it or deny the truth.

---

7  James 3:1.

> [15] Such "wisdom" does not come down from heaven but is earthly, unspiritual, demonic. [16] For where you have envy and selfish ambition, there you find disorder and every evil practice. [17] But the wisdom that comes from heaven is first of all pure; then peace-loving, considerate, submissive, full of mercy and good fruit, impartial and sincere. [18] Peacemakers who sow in peace reap a harvest of righteousness.[8]

Wisdom is shown by a good life. Wisdom from below is shown by envy and selfish ambition (reiterated twice!). The teaching gift is invigorated by a life of integrity.

The Bible warns against false teachers, just as it warns against false prophets. A false teacher may be someone who has the aptitude for teaching, but not the spiritual gift. Or a false teacher may be someone who has succumbed to envy and ambition. Second Peter 2 is an extended discourse against false teachers, and it opens with this warning:

> [1] But there were also false prophets among the people, just as there will be false teachers among you. They will secretly introduce destructive heresies, even denying the sovereign Lord who bought them—bringing swift destruction on themselves. [2] Many will follow their depraved conduct and will bring the way of truth into disrepute. [3] In their greed these teachers will exploit you with fabricated stories. Their condemnation has long been hanging over them, and their destruction has not been sleeping.[9]

---

8  James 3:13-18.

9  2 Peter 2:1-3.

The marks of a false teacher are they have two sets of rules: one for you and a different one for themselves. Their teaching is always to their benefit. Those with the gift of teaching must do a ruthless self-inventory to see if they are living what they teach and to make sure those they teach benefit more than themselves.

One further warning for those with the gift of teaching. Because they spend so much time with Scripture, they can become careless. The temptation will be to add to God's revelation or to take away from it. Teachers must remember this clear warning:

> [18] I warn everyone who hears the words of the prophecy of this scroll: If anyone adds anything to them, God will add to that person the plagues described in this scroll. [19] And if anyone takes words away from this scroll of prophecy, God will take away from that person any share in the tree of life and in the Holy City, which are described in this scroll.[10]

While this specifically applies to the book of Revelation, it is a warning about all scripture. Our temptation is to ignore uncomfortable passages and to claim a new insight by adding to scripture.

I once heard an engaging sermon on the Prodigal Son delivered by a well-known pastor. He told how the Prodigal Son had developed a taste for the food fed to the pigs. So after he returned to his father's house, he kept some hog slop hidden in a closet in his room. Late at night he would sneak into the closet and eat some of the slop, thus keeping his connection with his old way of life. The preacher then likened this behavior to the behavior of a Christian who has been saved

---

10  Revelation 22:18-19.

but continue to hold onto hidden sin. As I said, it was an engaging message. It only had one problem, and that was a big one. That story is not in the Bible. This preacher added to God's word for the sake of good message.

If you have the gift of teaching, bend yourself to the text; do not bend the text to suit you.

Above all, use your gift! Find someone to mentor, or a group to teach. Your gift of teaching grows as you exercise it!

## What this gift looks like in real life

I've been blessed to have some good teachers in my life. Some had the aptitude for teaching; the best teachers had the spiritual gift of teaching.

J.J. Owens was my teacher in seminary. He had the gift of teaching. A brilliant man, he graduated from college at age 16 and was fluent in 10 languages. Dr. Owens had a way of making Hebrew come alive. Though I was hardly a gifted linguist, I soaked up every class of his I could take.

One of my most profound learning experiences happened one day in his class. We were translating a chapter in Amos; there were 15 of us in class. He started on the far side of the room, and had the student seated in the first chair translate four verses of the passage we were studying. Then he pointed to the next student and had him translate the same four verses *without* using any of the words the first student used. The second student made it through with some creative effort. Dr. Owens pointed to the third student and told him to translate the same passage; only he was now prohibited from using any of the words the first two students had used.

Suddenly, the rest of the class was thrown into panic. We realized his intent. We were all to translate the passage, and we would not be able to repeat words already used. I did a quick count. I was number 14 in a class of 15. Panic set in.

I've never listened harder to recitations in class in my life. My mind raced through meanings of words and the intent of the author. When my time finally came, I translated the passage using the Southern vernacular I learned in my childhood. Dr. Owens beamed as I translated Amos 5:19, southern style:

> It'll be like a redneck running from a wildcat and then running into a mean sow bear,

> Then that same feller runs into his shack, leans against the wall, and a rattlesnake jumps out and bites him.

Dr. Owens taught us the flexibility of language that day, about digging for the true meaning of words, and about the nature of Scripture – that it was alive, dynamic, and powerful. He did it without lecture. He gave us an exercise that built a bridge so we would know what he knew. That day remains the best learning moment of my life.

Dr. Owens was a pipe. The force of his knowledge spread the life-giving water of Jesus a little further and my roots went a little further in seeking nourishment.

## Where from here

If you have the gift of teaching, dig deep into God's word. Don't assume you will get a revelation no one has ever had; assume God will lead you to share timeless truth in a way that will help people grow the roots of their lives toward Jesus. Start finding that person to mentor. Find that group to teach. Be the pipe that grows the roots.

# CHAPTER 5

# Feeding the Tree: Encouragement

As I shared in the last chapter, irrigation in the orange groves has changed. Now instead of putting down and picking up aluminum irrigation pipes, plastic hose runs down each row of trees. Under each tree are one or more micro-jets that spray water directly to the roots.

After this system of irrigation was put in place, researchers discovered that fertilizer could be liquefied and injected into the irrigation system. This would put the plant nutrients right to the roots. Instead of fertilizer being put out three or four times a year in granular form, it could be given to the trees on a weekly basis in small doses. Nutrients would come to the tree at a rate the tree could handle.

Now most wells in orange groves have a large plastic tank sitting nearby. A hose runs from the tank to the irrigation pipe. The water brings the fertilizer.

The spiritual gift of encouragement brings nutrition to the lives that are malnourished. If our analogy of the wells and trees can be applied, Jesus is the well of living water, dry and dying lives are the trees, Jesus followers are the pipes, and the Holy Spirit is the tank that holds the nutritional fertilizer. When the presence of Jesus is brought by His followers to dry and dying lives, it is also accompanied by the Holy Spirit, who works in concert with Jesus. People with the gift of encouragement are endowed with a special gift that brings the nourishment of the Spirit. Encouragers help people grow stronger and they help people bear more fruit.

## What is Encouragement?

In Romans 12:6-8, Paul listed the gifts of prophecy, service, and teaching. Continuing his idea that we all have gifts that differ according to the grace given us, he tells us to use each gift as it is intended to be used:

[8] if it is to encourage, then give encouragement;[1]

The Greek word used for encouragement is *Parakalon*. It is a compound word; *-kalon* is from the Greek word "to call;" and *Para-*, a preposition with a wide range of meaning. In this case it means "towards" or "to." Thus the first meaning of the word is "to call to." Over time, *parakalon* came to mean "to beseech," "to exhort,"[2] and "to comfort." These evolving meanings inform our understanding of the gift of encouragement.

An encourager beseeches, or asks for help with a sense of urgency. The need is critical and the moment for assistance to be given is now. The feeling is almost that of a court scene, where an encourager becomes

---

1  Romans 12:8.

2  Theological Dictionary of the New Testament, Vol. V, pp. 774-776.

an advocate for a client who is before the court. An encourager is an intercessor, pleading for those in authority to take action.

An encourager also exhorts. This is a winsome proclamation of good news that is meant to bring hope. Paul declares himself as this kind of ambassador:

> [20] We are therefore Christ's ambassadors, as though God were making His exhortation through us. We implore you on Christ's behalf: Be reconciled to God.[3]

When an encourager speaks, he or she is able to draw people toward Jesus. When they encourage people to live like Jesus, they are able to inspire a change in behavior. This work of encouragement is different than mere persuasion; it invites people to put their hope not in themselves but in Jesus. Encouragement is profoundly "grace-filled." It seeks to build up, not tear down. The goal of the encourager is salvation, not condemnation.

In the Roman army, an officer known as the "*paraclete*" was given the task of communicating with the troops. He would run right behind the front line of the battle, giving instructions, relaying news of the battle, and connecting the unit with other parts of the army. The idea was that troops would be encouraged by knowing what their commander wanted, and they would have hope because they would know they were not alone.

---

3   2 Corinthians 5:20, author's translation.

This is what an encourager does. His exhortations encourage people to move forward, to take new ground, and to believe that with God, all things are possible.

An encourager comforts. He or she is able to bring the gifts of God to someone whose heart is troubled. Encouragers provide gracious reminders that a person is not alone. By their physical presence they are able to bring the Spirit of God.[4]

In our culture, comfort is often misunderstood. We think comfort is sweetness and being nice. Sweetness is not a fruit of the Spirit, nor is "being nice." Jesus expands our understanding of comfort and encouragement when he describes the work of the Holy Spirit:

> [16] And I will ask the Father, and he will give you another advocate to help you and be with you forever— [17] the Spirit of truth. The world cannot accept him, because it neither sees him nor knows him. But you know him, for he lives with you and will be in you.[5]

> [26] But the Advocate, the Holy Spirit, whom the Father will send in my name, will teach you all things and will remind you of everything I have said to you.[6]

> [7] But very truly I tell you, it is for your good that I am going away. Unless I go away, the Advocate will not come to you; but if I go, I will send him to you. [8] When he comes, he will prove

---

4  Theological Dictionary of the New Testament, Vol. V, pp. 794-799.

5  John 14:16-17.

6  John 14:26.

the world to be in the wrong about sin and righteousness and judgment.[7]

[13] But when he, the Spirit of truth, comes, he will guide you into all the truth. He will not speak on his own; he will speak only what he hears, and he will tell you what is yet to come.[8]

The word translated "advocate" in these passages is the Greek word *parakleton* or *paraklete*. It means someone who does the work of *parakalon*. If you have the gift of encouragement, the work of the Holy Spirit is your guide in deploying your gift.

Like the Holy Spirit, an encourager is able to "be with" people whose lives are empty or people who are in crisis. They are able to do the ministry of presence, helping by simply being there.

Like the Holy Spirit, an encourager teaches and reminds people of what they already know. Just as the Holy Spirit helped men on the road to Emmaus remember everything Jesus had said to them after he broke bread, so an encourager is able to remind someone in crisis about a time when God was there for them. They are able to do so in a non-anxious, non-condemning way.

Like the Holy Spirit, an encourager helps people realize that something is wrong, that it is sin. An encourager is also able to help people see the consequences of their sin. We speak of people who are "the voice of conscience." They likely have the gift of encouragement and are able to clearly see sin. But like the Spirit, they are not oppressive;

---

7  John 16:7-8.

8  John 16:13.

rather, their voice urges a change of course. Encouragers can also help people realize what they are experiencing is a consequence of sin. The encourager must be careful here; not every bad thing that happens to a person is a consequence of sin. Someone with the true gift of encouragement, however, is able to discern when something bad is a result of sin. For example, if a man laments that his wife has left him and is suing him for divorce, someone with the gift of encouragement will be able to speak the truth and tell the man that the coming divorce is a result of his repeated unfaithfulness to his wife. He is experiencing the consequence of sin.

Finally, like the Holy Spirit, an encourager is able to guide people to the truth. Truth is better absorbed when it is discovered, rather than when it is imposed. Unlike a prophet, who tells, or a teacher who instructs, an encourager is able to orchestrate a conversation or a talk so people arrive at the truth themselves.

The Bible presents the gift of encouragement as the gift that is able to bring an empowering presence that advocates, exhorts, and comforts. When the gift is truly from God, it is shared in a way that moves people forward.

## Biblical Examples of the Gift of Encouragement

It is probable that Joshua had the gift of encouragement; he encouraged Moses as he led the difficult people of Israel through the wilderness. Later, when he assumed leadership of the nation, his method of leadership was one of encouragement. He assured the people of God they could defeat their enemies in battle if God was on their side.

Jonathan, the son of Saul, also likely had the gift of encouragement. When his friend David was sought by Saul so he could be put to death, Jonathan advocates for David, just as an encourager would do:

> [4] Jonathan spoke well of David to Saul his father and said to him, "Let not the king do wrong to his servant David; he has not wronged you, and what he has done has benefited you greatly.[9]

Joshua is paired with Moses; Jonathan is paired with David. Often the encourager is paired with someone who has gifts of leadership and prophecy; they enable the prophet or leader to function at a higher, more consistent level.

This pairing phenomenon happens again when a man named Barnabas is paired with Saul, who becomes Paul. In the book of Acts, Barnabas is introduced before Paul:

> [36] Joseph, a Levite from Cyprus, whom the apostles called Barnabas (which means "son of encouragement"), [37] sold a field he owned and brought the money and put it at the apostles' feet.[10]

Barnabas' nickname so described him, soon he was known as the "son of encouragement" instead of Joseph. Though born into a family that would have enabled him to serve in the Temple, he joins the Jesus movement as an early follower. Just as you would expect an encourager to do, he helped the movement by selling land and then giving the proceeds to the apostles.

---

9   1 Samuel 19:4.

10   Acts 4:36-37.

I can tell you from personal experience that as the leader of a group of Jesus followers, I am encouraged when someone knows a financial need and then shares a gift that meets that need! Giving can be energized as encouragement!

It is Barnabas that advocates for Saul/Paul after his conversion:

> [26] When he came to Jerusalem, he tried to join the disciples, but they were all afraid of him, not believing that he really was a disciple. [27] But Barnabas took him and brought him to the apostles. He told them how Saul on his journey had seen the Lord and that the Lord had spoken to him, and how in Damascus he had preached fearlessly in the name of Jesus. [28] So Saul stayed with them and moved about freely in Jerusalem, speaking boldly in the name of the Lord.[11]

By advocating for Paul, Barnabas opened the door for a changed man with the gift of teaching to begin sharing his gift.

News came to the church at Jerusalem that the Good News of Jesus was reaching non-Jewish people in Antioch. The leaders in Jerusalem sent Barnabas up to see what was happening. Naturally, Barnabas began encouraging believers right away:

> [22] News of this reached the church in Jerusalem, and they sent Barnabas to Antioch. [23] When he arrived and saw what the grace of God had done, he was glad and encouraged them all to remain true to the Lord with all their hearts. [24] He was a good

---

11  Acts 9:26-28.

man, full of the Holy Spirit and faith, and a great number of people were brought to the Lord.

²⁵ Then Barnabas went to Tarsus to look for Saul, ²⁶ and when he found him, he brought him to Antioch. So for a whole year Barnabas and Saul met with the church and taught great numbers of people. The disciples were called Christians first at Antioch.¹²

Encouragers offer their gift from a place of joy. They see God at work and their hearts rejoice! Barnabas became, for that new group of believers, a voice that reminded them to stay centered in Jesus. Luke, who wrote Acts, reminds us again that this extra-ordinary man was filled with the Spirit and faith. The gift of encouragement requires abiding in the Spirit, so as encouragement is given, encouragement is received.

Once again, Barnabas opens the door for Saul. Encouragers think, "Who can I find to share this fantastic opportunity?" No wonder the Holy Spirit later selects Barnabas and Saul/Paul for a special mission:

² While they were worshiping the Lord and fasting, the Holy Spirit said, "Set apart for me Barnabas and Saul for the work to which I have called them."¹³

Barnabas and Saul set off on a missionary journey to share Jesus with people who have never heard the Good News. Again God's pattern is seen: a teacher/prophet/leader paired with someone who has the gift of encouragement. Paul and Barnabas are able to share the story of

---

12  Acts 11:22-26.

13  Acts 13:2.

Jesus, start churches, and disciple new believers. Paul does the bulk of the teaching while Barnabas brings encouragement to Paul and those new in their faith.

One final story about Paul and Barnabas emphasizes how an encourager advocates for someone. Paul and Barnabas agree they need to return to check on the churches they established. Barnabas wants to take along John Mark, who had left them on the first trip. Paul did not want John Mark to go. Paul and Barnabas clashed:

> [39] They had such a sharp disagreement that they parted company. Barnabas took Mark and sailed for Cyprus, [40] but Paul chose Silas and left, commended by the believers to the grace of the Lord.[14]

This disagreement perfectly captures the tension that often exists between those with the gift of leadership and those with the gift of encouragement. Leaders define people in terms of their loyalty; encouragers define people in terms of possibilities. Who was right and who was wrong? Luke gives us no judgments; he simply is telling us how two people with two different gifts can see the same person, and see two different things. It didn't matter: trips were made, souls were saved, and the Kingdom of God marched on.

Encouragers like Barnabas advocate for people and help them find their way to serve God. Encouragers live close to the Spirit so they can receive encouragement even as they give encouragement. Encouragers open the doors so other people can share the joy of people finding

---

14   Acts 15:39-40.

Jesus. They are the pipes that bring not just water, but nutrients to people who do not yet know what they can do.

## Ways the gift of Encouragement is used

In a discouraging world, encouragement is the gift that helps a life to flourish, and in turn bear fruit. Paul tells us that we receive encouragement so we can give encouragement:

> [3] Praise be to the God and Father of our Lord Jesus Christ, the Father of compassion and the God of all comfort, [4] who comforts us in all our troubles, so that we can comfort those in any trouble with the comfort we ourselves receive from God. [5] For just as we share abundantly in the sufferings of Christ, so also our comfort abounds through Christ.[15]

The NIV translates *parakalon* here as "comfort." We are told we receive encouragement from God so we can encourage others. Church is to be a place of encouragement!

If you have the gift of encouragement, you may find yourself drawn to minister to those who are discouraged or are facing challenges. The best counselors I know have the gift of encouragement; they see possibilities. Like all the gifts, encouragement can be enhanced by education and training; but those with the true gift are able to help people move forward by helping them discover truth.

Encouragers are effective greeters to newcomers. It is a scary thing to come to a church for the first time. Everyone who comes to a worship service for the first time is wondering the same thing: "Is there anyone

---

15   2 Corinthians 1:3-5

here like me?" An encourager helps them feel welcomed and accepted. They help people find their tribe. They open doors to new friendships and relationships.

The gift of encouragement is needed by those who experience a chronic condition they cannot change. People who have health problems, who are shut-in, and who are incarcerated need encouragement. They need hope brought to them. Encouragers lift the spirits of those who face daily struggles.

People in a crisis need encouragement. The circumstances of their situation blinds them to hope. They cannot see God's plan or God's hand. A crisis may put someone in the hospital. They need a visit that brings them hope. They need prayers of hope.

A family may face a crisis in marriage or with a child. They need an encourager to bring hope. When couples in crisis come to see me, they are so caught up in despair, they often see divorce as the only option. Sometimes I will ask them to tell me about when they met and when they started dating. They begin to tell their story and their mood shifts. They are being reminded of what they already knew: there was a reason they fell in love; they simply lost sight of the reason. The gift of encouragement guides them to the truth they already know. In a crisis, people need to be helped to know what they already know.

Encouragers are effective intercessors. They see possibilities for people. They are able to pray a new vision for life: for a drug addict to live a life of recovery; for a depressed woman to find joy; for a single Mom to forgive her ex.

Because encouragement includes advocacy, those with the gift often advocate for those who have no voice. They want to help orphans and victims of sex trafficking; they want justice for the poor and inclusion for the excluded. They feel a righteous anger when people are discriminated against because of race or economic status. Encouragers see different possibilities for all the down-trodden in the world.

Because encouragers can see possibilities, they are excellent recruiters. They can see what others can accomplish with their gifts and they want them to succeed. When a need presents itself, unlike people with the gift of service who think of how they can help, an encourager thinks about who can meet the need and discover the joy of serving.

When a person has both the encouragement gift and the teaching gift they are excellent mentors. Not only do they like to teach; they like to see others succeed.

The Biblical pattern shows us another role an encourager will often take: they are paired with a leader or a prophet. This pairing, like Barnabas and Paul, can do great things together. Encouragers are effective in the second chair in organizations. For example, a teacher may be effective in conveying truth, but he or she might need an encourager to bring hope to people in the group.

Because encouragement is not as visible as other spiritual gifts, it can be overlooked as churches structure their ministries. This is a mistake. Churches need to provide channels for this gift to be shared. Encouragement is the pipe that brings hope to discouraged people!

## You might have the gift of Encouragement if:

- You can bring hope to people.
- You have a passion to advocate for the poor and the disadvantaged.
- You help people discover what they can do.
- You find more joy in giving someone else an opportunity to serve than serving yourself.
- You see possibilities of who people can become in Christ.
- You like seeing people make progress.
- You are named by someone as their voice of conscience and they appreciate you in that role.
- You enjoy lifting up a leader.
- You encourage others and it energizes you; it doesn't drain you.

## What to do if you have this gift

To find out if you have the gift of encouragement, pay attention to people you interact with. If they respond positively to time spent with you, you may well have this gift. The gift of encouragement, unlike some of the other gifts, requires no platform. It requires someone to encourage!

The gift of encouragement is enhanced when encouragers understand how their gift works. Spend time reflecting on how you impact people. Think about the encouragement process: how you recognize discouragement, how you evaluate a need, and how you move toward a person. Notice when your heart stirs. It may be helpful to keep a journal of moments when you deploy your gift so you can begin to see how the gift will be used in your particular calling.

Because most encouragers find it natural to encourage and because they often are bored with organization, they seldom build a system of encouragement. This is a mistake. Encouragement harnessed to structure helps encouragement to be deployed at the right time. Just like fertilizer is now distributed at closer intervals, encouragement offered more frequently but at lower strength brings a source of nourishment to discouraged lives that they can count on.

For example, someone with the gift of encouragement and a calling to work with senior adults may decide to visit a nursing home. They really enjoy being with the people there and can see the impact their gift brings. Now imagine the impact of the encourager if they deploy their gift systematically; instead of haphazardly going by the nursing home, imagine if they scheduled one hour each week to use their gift. Now the nourishment of encouragement is given on a regular basis.

Encouragers would do well to learn all they can about how people operate. Studying psychology and sociology enhances their gift. When the insights from these fields are integrated with scriptural truth, a powerful spiritual synergy is born.

As you develop your gift of encouragement, open the door for others. Never use your gift alone! If you greet, recruit a partner. If you visit, invite someone to go with you. If you advocate for a group, form a team. Open the door for others to use their gifts.

The proof this gift is fully developed is when the encourager is mentoring mentors. Every mentor needs someone to mentor them, someone to encourage them. Encouragers should look for a leader who is doing too much and offer to come alongside. That's encouragement!

Encouragement ultimately is caring leadership. It is opening doors, lifting up the discouraged, and seeing God's possibilities for people

## What this gift looks like in real life

Larry is one of the finest encouragers I've ever known. In the twenty years I've known him, he over and over reminds me to keep perspective. Once early in my tenure as pastor of our church, we walked out of the church building following a rather contentious Stewardship Committee meeting. I looked at him and said, "That was tough." Larry laughed, and said, "Remember Clay, there are a lot of people who can figure what happened to the money after the fact. There are not too many who make things happen." His words that night lifted my soul.

For a number of years, Larry would call me during his morning walk – usually about 5:00 AM! Thankfully he would call the office phone and leave me a voice mail. His messages always started with, "God loves you and so do I."

When Larry served on the Vision Council at our church, he was always the one who wanted to know how I was doing. He asked me about my family and about my children. He knew my family was closest to my heart.

Once, Larry asked me where I most felt the presence of God. I told him that I most felt God's presence on my boat. He replied, "Then Clay, spend as much time as possible on your boat! We need you to be as close to God as possible." Like a good encourager, he guided me to the truth I needed to know, then gave me permission to live that truth.

Larry understands leadership is lonely. When I've had burdens about family or finances or even which truck to buy, Larry has been there. He has the gift of encouragement. He has been the Spirit of God to me, and I am forever grateful.

## Where from here

If you have this gift, or if you think you have it, don't be shy! You are a pipe, plugged into the Holy Spirit, joining with Jesus to bring the nourishment of hope to dry and dying lives. Encourage! Advocate! Help! Comfort! Recruit! Mentor! Visit! Lift up people and bring them hope!

CHAPTER 6

# The Mainline: Giving

When water leaves the well, it enters a large pipe called the mainline. The mainline usually stretches across all the rows of the orange grove, either length-wise or width-wise. Attached to the mainline are smaller lateral lines which carry the water on down to each section of the grove. Take away the mainline, and all other pipes are no good. If the mainline is too small, it can't carry enough water to reach the end of the far row of trees. If there's a crack in the mainline, the pressure falls and water winds up spilling out in the wrong place. The mainline doesn't directly serve the tree; it helps all the other pipes do their job. It takes an intact mainline for the irrigation system to do its job.

The spiritual gift of giving is like a mainline in an irrigation system. These special pipes, usually sized a bit larger than the lateral pipes, make sure the life-giving water gets to the trees. Giving makes sure other gifts can be deployed. People with other gifts depend on those with the gift of giving. Their generosity meets a need. Without this spiritual gift strongly engaged, people with other gifts are frustrated. Their constant comment: "If only we had the resources! We could – preach more, serve more, teach more, encourage more." The gift of giving is the mainline for the other gifts.

## What is Giving?

In Romans 12:8b, Paul breaks the pattern of his list of spiritual gifts. He has been following a simple outline: if you have the gift of prophecy, prophesy! If you have the gift of service, serve! If you have the gift of teaching, teach! If you have the gift of encouragement, encourage! Now he writes:

> If it is giving, then give generously.

Why does Paul break the pattern? I think the pattern is broken because Paul knows that all followers of Jesus are to give. Jesus said,

> [38] Give, and it will be given to you. A good measure, pressed down, shaken together and running over, will be poured into your lap. For with the measure you use, it will be measured to you.[1]

When Paul began to address this spiritual gift, he knew people would be tempted to say, "I don't have the gift of giving; therefore, I don't have to give." The spiritual gift of giving is different from the responsibility of giving.

Jesus gives to all of his followers the responsibility of giving. He does this because he knows giving grows our souls. When we give, we are more like God, who gave His only Son that we might live. When we give, we directly attack the selfishness of our hearts. When we give, we are counter-cultural, declaring our happiness not to be dependent on a lifestyle but on our Savior. When we give, we see God's super-natural provision.

---

1  Luke 6:38.

Giving is a key discipline of faith that every Christ follower must embrace as we follow Jesus. What then, is the spiritual gift of giving?

Paul uses two key words in Romans 12:8. The first is *metadidous.* It means to give or to impart. The picture of this word is simple: a person takes what they have and they give to someone else. The true spiritual gift of giving is done not with the expectation of reward, recognition, or return. It is an act of love.[2]

The second key word is *aploteti.* This word carries ideas of "free from inner discord," "innocent," "upright," and "pure." Here, as in 2 Corinthians 8:2, 9:11 and 9:13 it is often translated as "generously," with the idea of a sacrificially liberality.[3]

Describing this spiritual gift, Paul wants us to understand the distinction of the responsibility of giving and the gift of giving. People who have this gift give with a pure heart, not out of fear or hope of reward. There is no hint of "give so you will be blessed." There is purity of motive, sacrifice, and liberality.

When Paul writes to Jesus followers in Corinth, he urges them to take an offering that can be used for fellow Jesus followers in Jerusalem. He offers for an example the believers in Macedonia:

> [1]And now, brothers and sisters, we want you to know about the grace that God has given the Macedonian churches. [2] In the midst of a very severe trial, their overflowing joy and their extreme poverty welled up in rich generosity. [3] For I testify that

---

2   Theological Dictionary of the New Testament, Vol. II, p. 166.

3   Theological Dictionary of the New Testament, Vol. I, pp. 386-387.

they gave as much as they were able, and even beyond their ability. Entirely on their own, [4] they urgently pleaded with us for the privilege of sharing in this service to the Lord's people. [5] And they exceeded our expectations: They gave themselves first of all to the Lord, and then by the will of God also to us. [6] So we urged Titus, just as he had earlier made a beginning, to bring also to completion this act of grace on your part. [7] But since you excel in everything—in faith, in speech, in knowledge, in complete earnestness and in the love we have kindled in you—see that you also excel in this grace of giving.

[8] I am not commanding you, but I want to test the sincerity of your love by comparing it with the earnestness of others.[4]

Paul gives us marks of the gift of giving. First, the gift of giving is not based on what you have, but on your spirit. The Macedonians gave not out of abundance, but out of their poverty. There is an old preacher riddle about this principle: when is $40 more than $400? When a person making $400 a week puts $40 in the offering plate, and a person making $8,000 a week puts in $400. Generosity is not measured by amount, but by percentage.

A second mark of the gift of giving is that the gift is given voluntarily. People with the gift of giving initiate giving. They do not wait to be asked. According to Paul, the Macedonians begged to give. Whenever I witness someone begging to give, I know they have the gift of giving.

---

4  2 Corinthians 8:1-8.

A third mark of the gift of giving is that the gift is directed to God. It is giving to the cause of the Kingdom, not for honor or recognition. The giver begins by asking "God, what do you want me to do?"

A fourth mark of the gift of giving is that it sets an example. The Macedonians set the example for the Corinthians. Paul had no hesitation revealing what one group of people was giving to another group. The mark of true generosity is the example that is set.

The final mark of the gift of giving is that it is not commanded or coerced. Those with the gift of giving offer their gifts because of the love in their hearts, not because they are forced.

Paul teaches further about the gift of giving in the next chapter:

> [6] Remember this: Whoever sows sparingly will also reap sparingly, and whoever sows generously will also reap generously. [7] Each of you should give what you have decided in your heart to give, not reluctantly or under compulsion, for God loves a cheerful giver. [8] And God is able to bless you abundantly, so that in all things at all times, having all that you need, you will abound in every good work. [9] As it is written:

> "They have freely scattered their gifts to the poor;
>   their righteousness endures forever."

> [10] Now he who supplies seed to the sower and bread for food will also supply and increase your store of seed and will enlarge the harvest of your righteousness. [11] You will be enriched in every

way so that you can be generous on every occasion, and through us your generosity will result in thanksgiving to God.

[12] This service that you perform is not only supplying the needs of the Lord's people but is also overflowing in many expressions of thanks to God. [13] Because of the service by which you have proved yourselves, others will praise God for the obedience that accompanies your confession of the gospel of Christ, and for your generosity in sharing with them and with everyone else.[5]

Paul is teaching us that the gift of giving is unique because it has a multiplying effect. The more that is given, the more that is reaped. Those with the gift of giving, give cheerfully. They find joy in giving.

Givers see God providing. God gives them blessings in abundance so givers have enough to share. A true giver understands himself or herself as a steward. They know God has given them everything; He generously allows them to keep some and give some. Most people with the gift of giving are past the idea of "mine."

Finally, those with the gift of giving see other people blessed because of their gifts. Their gifts are a confession of their faith. People give thanks to God because people with the gift of giving are God's answers to their prayers.

## Biblical Examples of the Gift of Giving

In Genesis, God told Abraham to leave his father's house and go to a land and He would show him. When he arrived, God told him what would happen:

---

5   2 Corinthians 9:6-13.

² "I will make you into a great nation,
  and I will bless you;
I will make your name great,
  and you will be a blessing.
³ I will bless those who bless you,
  and whoever curses you I will curse;
and all peoples on earth
  will be blessed through you."⁶

From the beginning, Abraham was told he was being blessed so he could be a blessing. As he shared the blessings of God, others would be blessed.

In Genesis 14, Abraham's nephew Lot was caught in a battle between warring kings and was captured. When Abraham heard about this, he gathered the 318 men who were under his care and set out to recapture his nephew. After a long journey, he made a night attack, recovering Lot and all the other people and loot that had been captured. It was a stunning victory.

As he passed near the city of Jerusalem, the king of that city came out to bless him:

Then Melchizedek king of Salem brought out bread and wine. He was priest of God Most High, ¹⁹ and he blessed Abram, saying,

"Blessed be Abram by God Most High,
  Creator of heaven and earth.

---

6 Genesis 12:2-3.

> [20] And praise be to God Most High,
>    who delivered your enemies into your hand."

Then Abram gave him a tenth of everything.[7]

The King, Melchizedek, was also a priest. He blessed Abraham (known as Abram at this time), and in response Abraham gave him ten percent of everything.

Why did Abraham do this? It couldn't have been out of guilt; he had no previous interaction with Melchizedek. It couldn't have been out of pity; Melchizedek had not been involved in the battle. It couldn't have been out of obligation; Abraham owed Melchizedek nothing.

Abraham gave a tenth of everything as an act of worship. He was expressing gratitude to God for blessing him. Melchizedek offers the blessing of God, and in return, Abraham gives a blessing. People with the gift of giving give joyful gifts because they have a profound sense of being blessed.

This is the first mention in the Bible of percentage giving. Abraham gives ten percent. Why? This had not been mandated by God. Abraham understands giving is not a tax, but a privilege. Ten percent is a significant amount to display gratitude.

Abraham teaches us that givers give in response to being blessed; they give as an act of worship; and they give a significant percentage to show their gratitude.

Jesus called attention to a woman who had the gift of giving:

---

7  Genesis 14:18-20.

"[41] Jesus sat down opposite the place where the offerings were put and watched the crowd putting their money into the temple treasury. Many rich people threw in large amounts. [42] But a poor widow came and put in two very small copper coins, worth only a few cents.

[43] Calling his disciples to him, Jesus said, "Truly I tell you, this poor widow has put more into the treasury than all the others. [44] They all gave out of their wealth; but she, out of her poverty, put in everything—all she had to live on."[8]

Jesus contrasted this woman's gift to rich people who were putting in large amounts. In doing so, he reminds us that the gift of giving is not determined by the size of the gift, but by the proportion of the gift to one's wealth.

The widow was remarkable in her generosity. Her spiritual gift of giving led her to give everything. The mark of a fully matured gift of giving is faith that God will provide. The widow is able to give all because she trusts God for all.

The widow teaches givers to trust God with everything. There is a great freedom in this. Anxieties about financial security go away. They are replaced by a deep trust in God's love and care. This kind of trust is available to all who grow their gift of giving, regardless of their assets.

---

8  Mark 12:41-44.

## Ways the gift of Giving is used

I was at Walmart early one morning to get some groceries. In line ahead of me was a young mom, in pajama bottoms and a jacket, holding her bundled up baby. She was trying to buy a jug of milk and a box of cereal. I couldn't help but watch her interchange with the cashier. It was clear she didn't speak English and didn't have enough money to purchase two simple items. I had a God whisper in that moment: "Pay for her items." I spoke up, telling the cashier that I would pay for her groceries. The cashier gave the coins back to the woman, pointed at me, and then waved her on. The woman turn to me, smiled, and then gathered her groceries and left.

I'd like to tell you I did that because I have the gift of giving. I don't. But in the line that day, as God whispered to me, I remembered this was the kind of thing my step-father would do without hesitation. He had the gift of giving.

The most powerful impact someone with the gift of giving has is the example they set. They remind those of us without the gift that we are to share and be generous.

Givers provide resources so the work of Jesus can be done. The inescapable reality is God's work requires resources. Many idealist movements have been launched in the name of Jesus declaring they will not need money. After a few months, those movements either get serious about finances or they wither away. God decided that his work would require earthly resources.

When givers give, they enable God's work to be done. Food can be bought for the hungry. Children can be taught God's word. Buildings can be built, to be used as tools for God's work. Churches can hire staff, so full time attention can be given to the doing of God's work. Missionaries are sent to tell others about Jesus. Prisoners are taught the scripture. Technology can be purchased so the Good News can be heard by many more.

Givers are able to open doors of opportunity for God's work. When a piece of land came up for sale near a downtown church, a gentleman in that church realized the church needed the property to expand. He also realized the church did not have the resources to purchase the property on hand. Given the fast changing real estate market, he also knew that to call a church business meeting and discuss purchasing the property would guarantee a bidding war for the property. He had the resources to purchase the property and give it to the church, so he did. He helped the church open the door to the future by using his gift of giving.

People with the spiritual gift of giving understand they have been blessed to be a blessing, just like Abraham. No matter how much they have, or how little they have, they see every resource as a blessing.

Mrs. Horn was an older widow in my church in Kentucky. She lived in a ram-shackled older farmhouse on a limited fixed income. Every Monday, I picked her up for a ladies Bible study I taught. This caused no gossip; she was 82 and I was 28. She knew we were trying to raise money for new hymnals in the church; and fundraising had been slow.

One Monday morning she got into my truck, and then pressed into my hand a dirty handkerchief filled with coins and loose bills. I asked her what this was for, and she told me she had received an unexpected

Medicare reimbursement check. The coins and bills in the handkerchief were her tithe of her check. I began to protest, telling her she didn't need to tithe on a reimbursement check. She looked at me through her thick glasses and said, "Now Clay, God has blessed me. I want to give this and I want it go toward the hymnals. Plus, I'm an old woman, and you'll do what I tell you to do!"

I took the handkerchief, feeling like I was handling one of the most sacred objects I'd ever held. I made sure the money was put in the hymnal fund. I also realized that day I was in the presence of one of God's great givers.

Givers are not merely generous with money. One family I know that has this gift shares their beach condo, free of charge, with pastors who need a rest. Another family with the gift of giving and service is the away from church headquarters for the student ministry. Their big back room and their pool make their home an ideal attractional place for students. One man I know with the gift of giving owned a plane; he flew his pastor to speak at conferences and to find staff.

People with the gift of giving know they are blessed to be a blessing!

### You might have the gift of Giving if:
- You see the needs of people and it moves you to provide so those needs can be met.
- God has blessed you with abundant resources.
- You are able to see a need before most people recognize it.
- You write a check or make an electronic transfer to God's work, your heart is filled with joy.
- You often feel led to make a spontaneous gift to meet a need.

- People praise you for being generous.
- Your generosity inspires others.
- You give before you are asked.
- You think in terms of "How much can I give" not "How much do I have to give?"
- Your giving is not just spontaneous but regular and systematic.
- You prefer not to be recognized for your giving.
- The majority of your giving is not to non-profits organizations but to the work of Jesus and His church.

## What to do if you have this gift

This spiritual gift is rather easy to deploy. Give.

If you have the spiritual gift of giving, chances are you already give something. You have already stepped into the joy of giving. It may be, however, that you have not begun to give to God's body, the church. Step in and start giving something to God's work.

The next step for you is to step up your giving. Begin to give ten percent of your income. The Bible is clear that this is an expectation God has for us. Giving ten percent is a reminder that God owns everything; thus we bring the tithe, we do not give the tithe:

> [10] Bring the whole tithe into the storehouse, that there may be food in my house. Test me in this," says the Lord Almighty, "and see if I will not throw open the floodgates of heaven and pour out so much blessing that there will not be room enough to store it.[9]

---

9  Malachi 3:10, underline added by author.

Giving ten percent teaches us to be systematic in giving. Just as the gifts of service and encouragement grow when they shift from spontaneous moments to regular deployment, the gift of giving is strengthened when it is done in in a systematic, regular way.

In my opinion, to step into giving and to step up to tithing are first steps for those with the gift of giving. They prepare givers for the final step – stepping out in faith, like the widow.

To step out in faith is to give more than the expected and to feel joyful, not fearful. I know people with the gift of giving who share 40% of their income. They give ten percent regularly to their church, and then give liberally to missions and other Christian organizations. They give to individuals without worrying about the tax write-off.

Because givers are generous people, they are often blessed with exceptional financial management skills. They are able to advise others on investments and allocation of resources. Several givers I know excel at developing plans that help families get out of debt and get on firmer financial ground. These givers are giving not only their money, but their financial wisdom.

Once you realize you have the gift of giving, you are quickly able to step into giving something; to step up to giving ten percent; and then to step out and give generously. If you are new to the faith, or new to the idea that your gift requires use, your lifestyle may require adjustment. Never let your lifestyle keep you from using your gift. David Platt tells of a conviction in this area, when he chose to move from a larger house to a smaller house, so he could give more.

I find people with the gift of giving are sometimes ashamed that this gift is their strength. I was talking once with one of our church members, Glenn, who asked me to help him find his purpose. I asked Glenn what he was good at doing. Glenn told me in all the years he had been in church he had served, but had never enjoyed it.

"Please don't ask me to usher, I'm not comfortable meeting people I don't know," he said. "And for heaven's sake, don't ask me to teach a class or sing in the choir. I hate to speak in front of people and I can't sing. If you put me on the Finance Team, I'll leave the church."

I couldn't help but laugh. I knew Glenn well enough that I knew he was joking. I also knew him well enough that I knew he was partly serious.

I said to Glenn, "You've told me things you're not good at. What are you good at?" He thought for a moment, and then he said, "I'm good at making money. That's my talent. That's what God helps me to do."

I told Glenn I thought his purpose in life was to make all the money he could and to give as much of it away as possible. A big smile came upon his face, and he said, "I can do that for God." Until he passed away, he made money, gave money away, and helped amazing things happen for God.

If you have the gift of giving, use it. Bring others joy!

## What this gift looks like in real life

I've known some great givers in my life. I can't tell about some them because they are still living. They would be embarrassed if I called them by name. God blessed them and they blessed others by their generosity. But there are two great givers I'd like to tell you about, and two folks that break my heart.

Truett Cathy, the founder of Chick-Fil-A had the gift of giving. Enormously successful in business, he enjoyed the benefits of wealth, but he enjoyed sharing the blessings more. Truett tithed to his church, but he also established college scholarships, camps for kids, places for pastors to get away and recharge, and a host of other Kingdom enterprises. As his business grew, his giving grew. Ken Blanchard was so inspired by Truett Cathy, he wrote a book describing a truly successful life, based on Cathy's life.[10] Truett Cathy understood he was blessed to be a blessing. He was a mainline pipe that brought resources to other pipes so God's work could be done.

A second great giver I have known was my step-father, Lawrence. Lawrence came into my life when I was eight. He married my mother, who had been widowed. I knew Lawrence was generous when he bought me milkshakes that my mother wouldn't allow me to have!

I remember every Sunday Lawrence writing out a tithe check. This was a step of faith because we only got about 8 checks a year from selling oranges and cattle. Yet Lawrence trusted that God would provide. In our home church, when the preacher needed a new car, Lawrence would talk to a couple of other church members, they would come up with the money, and the preacher would get a new car.

But Lawrence was not generous with just money. When our cousin Willard was done picking watermelons from his field (usually about 200 acres – which is a big field!), Lawrence would take the truck and

---

10   Ken Blanchard and Truett Cathy, <u>The Generosity Factor.</u>

me and say, "I hate to see those watermelons go to waste. Let's go get a couple." A "couple of watermelons" would turn into 77 piled on the back of a Ford pick-up. We would stop at every widow's house in our community of Lemon Grove and drop off four or five melons.

Lawrence would see young ladies come to church dressed in old clothes and he would arrange for them to shop at the local dress store. The girls never knew where their new clothes came from. Lawrence saw needs, and he wanted to meet them, because he knew God had blessed him. He was a mainline pipe that brought resources to other pipes so God's work could be done.

There are two people I believe could have been great givers, but they never embraced the gift God had for them.

The story of one is found in the Bible:

> [17] As Jesus started on his way, a man ran up to him and fell on his knees before him. "Good teacher," he asked, "what must I do to inherit eternal life?"

> [18] "Why do you call me good?" Jesus answered. "No one is good—except God alone. [19] You know the commandments: 'You shall not murder, you shall not commit adultery, you shall not steal, you shall not give false testimony, you shall not defraud, honor your father and mother.'"

> [20] "Teacher," he declared, "all these I have kept since I was a boy."

<sup>21</sup> Jesus looked at him and loved him. "One thing you lack," he said. "Go, sell everything you have and give to the poor, and you will have treasure in heaven. Then come, follow me."

<sup>22</sup> At this the man's face fell. He went away sad, because he had great wealth.[11]

Every time I read this story, it breaks my heart. This rich young man could have been in Jesus' hall of fame of faith. He could have been a great giver. But he loved money more than he loved the gift of giving that had been placed before him. It's sad when people waste their resources on themselves.

I knew a man just like this rich young man, except he was a rich old man. God had begun to work in his life and he had returned to the faith of his childhood. He made the decision to join our church and then offered to take me to lunch. Over lunch he asked me about tithing. I explained it the best I could. I told him that God had probably blessed him with all his resources so he could begin to know the joy of giving. He looked uncomfortable, and changed the subject.

A few months later, the rich old man suffered a stroke and passed away. When he died, he had given nothing to God's church, to the work of Jesus.

Whenever I think about that man, it breaks my heart. He died with his fortune intact and his gift unused. He was a mainline pipe that finally connected to the well, but never connected to the other pipes under the trees.

---

11  Mark 10:17-22.

## Where from here

If you have this gift, give systematically over ten percent. When you see a need you can meet, meet it! As God blesses you, share it! Go to a church leader and tell them "I have the gift of giving and I have some resources that need giving. Where is it needed?" Embrace the joy of knowing your gifts will make a difference forever.

Pat Neff became very wealthy and gave much of his fortune to Baylor University. Then he was wiped out in the Great Depression and lost most of his money. Someone asked him if he regretted giving so much of his fortune away. "No!" he replied. "All the money I kept for myself I lost. All the money I gave away will have eternal impact."

That's the way a giver thinks and lives. They are a mainline pipe.

CHAPTER 7

# Valves: Leadership

Every irrigation system is governed by special pipes called valves. Valves have a handle or knob that lowers a disc into the pipe, stopping the flow of water. When the pipe is sealed the water flows in a different direction. By opening and closing different valves water is directed to a specific section of the orange grove or down a specific row of trees. The valves may be clustered close to the well or they may be along the mainline. The valves put the water where it is needed most.

This is what the gift of leadership does. People with the gift of leadership are able to discern the condition of a group or organization and direct the life giving Good News of Jesus to the place where it is most needed. This means leaders make decisions, mindful of consequences, so the whole church family can benefit.

## What is Leadership?

The first four gifts are presented in a simple pattern: if you have the gift, do the gift. Paul breaks the pattern with the gift of giving and sets a new pattern for the last three gifts. The gifts are named and instruction is given about how the gift should be applied. For example, in the previous chapter, Paul told those with the gift of giving to give generously. Now he says to those with the gift of leadership:

> [8c]if it is to lead, do it diligently.[1]

The word translated "lead" is the Greek word *proistamenos*. It means "to go first, to preside, to lead, to conduct, to direct, and to govern." In the Bible, it refers to a work of love, whereby a leader loves those behind him or her and wants to help them succeed.[2]

The word translated "diligently" is the Greek word *spoude.* It carries the idea of "energetic diligence." Those with the gift of leadership bring energy to whatever they lead. They are not easily distracted or dissuaded from the goals of the organization.

To lead is to accept responsibility for the flock of God. Thus those who lead well are honored, especially if their gift of leadership is matched with gifts of prophecy and teaching:

> [17] The elders who direct the affairs of the church well are worthy of double honor, especially those whose work is preaching and teaching.[3]

Paul reminds the entire church that leadership is not optional; it is essential for the church. This is the gift that gets things done. It's the valve that directs that water.

---

1 Romans 12:8c.

2 Theological Dictionary of the New Testament, Vol. VI pp. 700-701.

3 1 Timothy 5:17.

## Biblical Examples of the Gift of Leadership

The Bible offers different images of this gift: some leaders are entrepreneurs, starting something new, like Abraham. Some are shepherds, guiding God's people on a journey to a new pasture, like Moses. Deborah was a leader who made decisions. David was a general who led soldiers into battle. Daniel led through wisdom, advising the King. The gift of leadership has many expressions, but one central theme. All these leaders were directing the energy of God where it was needed most.

Often the toughest leadership job is to follow the exceptional leader. Two men in the Bible were given this assignment. The Spirit also gave them the gift of leadership.

Joshua apprenticed under Moses. When Moses died, God spoke to Joshua:

> After the death of Moses the servant of the Lord, the Lord said to Joshua son of Nun, Moses' aide: [2] "Moses my servant is dead. Now then, you and all these people, get ready to cross the Jordan River into the land I am about to give to them—to the Israelites. [3] I will give you every place where you set your foot, as I promised Moses. [4] Your territory will extend from the desert to Lebanon, and from the great river, the Euphrates—all the Hittite country—to the Mediterranean Sea in the west. [5] No one will be able to stand against you all the days of your life. As I was with Moses, so I will be with you; I will never leave you nor forsake you. [6] Be strong and courageous, because you will

lead these people to inherit the land I swore to their ancestors to give them.[4]

When God gives the gift of leadership, he tells the recipient to face reality. Joshua must face the reality that Moses, the greatest leader in Israel's history, is dead. The mission, however, remains. God never gives the gift of leadership with also making the mission clear.

Those who receive the gift of leadership also receive a promise from God: He will be with them. He will empower them. He will help them accomplish what He calls them to do. God gives this unique promise to leaders because to lead means to risk. To every decision there is a potential positive and a potential negative. God's promise brings reassurance.

Leaders are told by God to look to God's equipping of leaders in the past. "As I was with Moses, so I will be with you." It's no accident that most people with the leadership gift are interested in history; they want to learn from great leaders of the past.

Joshua is also told to expect fear. "Be strong and courageous," he is told. Why would you need to tell someone this except for the possibility he or she may not be strong or courageous? Fear is the companion of leaders. Often, they are afraid of the consequences of decisions, or they are afraid of how they will hurt people, or they are afraid they will let down the people they lead.

The mark of those truly gifted by the spirit as leaders is they lead people toward a promise, God's inheritance, towards hope. Joshua is told

---

4  Joshua 1:1-6

the inheritance is there, across the Jordan River. He led the people across the river and to the promise of God.

You probably have heard about Joshua's initial success. After marching around the city of Jericho seven days, the walls of the city fall down and the first victory is notched.[5] But the second victory doesn't come as easily. The small town of Ai is attacked and the Israelites are defeated. Something is wrong and Joshua, the leader, has to find out what it is. It turns out one of the soldiers, Achan, kept some of the treasure for himself, instead of giving it to God.[6]

This is the tough part of being a leader. Everyone you lead has a mind of their own. You can give clear instructions and they can chose to ignore you and the instructions. Then you have to discover the problem and fix it, even though you didn't cause it.

Joshua made another mistake when he trusts the Gibeonites. They came pretending to be from far away and ask for peace. In reality, they lived in the land God promised to Israel. Joshua fails to do his due diligence and makes a treaty with them. When he finds out the truth, he must stick by his promise.[7] Leaders live with the consequences of their bad decisions.

Despite his failures, Joshua effectively leads Israel to conquer the Promised Land and substantially fulfill the mission God gave him. Everyone with the gift of leadership will experience stumbles on the way to ultimate success.

---

5  Joshua 6.

6  Joshua 7.

7  Joshua 9.

James, the brother of Jesus, had to follow his brother in leadership of the Jesus followers in Jerusalem. He was following the greatest leader who ever lived! At first, James did not believe his brother;[8] only later would he come to believe. Even though Peter at first has been the leader of the Jesus followers in Jerusalem, by 50 A.D. James is clearly the one who leads this church:

> [13]When they finished, James spoke up. "Brothers," he said, "listen to me. [14] Simon has described to us how God first intervened to choose a people for his name from the Gentiles.

> [19] "It is my judgment, therefore, that we should not make it difficult for the Gentiles who are turning to God.[9]

Though Peter, Paul, and Barnabas are all present at this meeting, it is James who takes the lead. Leaders must take the lead even when those with different strong gifts are present. Peter had the gift of prophecy, Paul the gift of teaching, and Barnabas the gift of the encouragement, but James leads the group to a decision point and a plan of action.

James is a valve; he is directing God's people, who also have gifts, in a specific direction.

When Paul returns to Jerusalem, he meets with James and the other elders of the church. They praise him for his ministry (important work for a leader!), warn him of a potential problem and they offer a solution:

---

8  Mark 3:21.

9  Acts 15:13-14, 19.

[18] The next day Paul and the rest of us went to see James, and all the elders were present. [19] Paul greeted them and reported in detail what God had done among the Gentiles through his ministry.

[20] When they heard this, they praised God. Then they said to Paul: "You see, brother, how many thousands of Jews have believed, and all of them are zealous for the law. [21] They have been informed that you teach all the Jews who live among the Gentiles to turn away from Moses, telling them not to circumcise their children or live according to our customs. [22] What shall we do? They will certainly hear that you have come, [23] so do what we tell you. There are four men with us who have made a vow. [24] Take these men, join in their purification rites and pay their expenses, so that they can have their heads shaved. Then everyone will know there is no truth in these reports about you, but that you yourself are living in obedience to the law. [25] As for the Gentile believers, we have written to them our decision that they should abstain from food sacrificed to idols, from blood, from the meat of strangled animals and from sexual immorality."

[26] The next day Paul took the men and purified himself along with them. Then he went to the temple to give notice of the date when the days of purification would end and the offering would be made for each of them.[10]

Even Paul recognizes the wisdom of James and the elder's counsel. He submits himself to it because he recognizes their gift of leadership.

---

10   Acts 21:18-26.

A few years later, Paul would write to Timothy, his protégé', and give instructions for those with the gift of leadership in the office of a leader:

> [4] He must manage his own family well and see that his children obey him, and he must do so in a manner worthy of full respect. [5] (If anyone does not know how to manage his own family, how can he take care of God's church?)[11]

Although the NIV translates the word *proistamenos* here as "manage," it is the same word used in Romans 12:8. The verse is better understood to read:

> He (the overseer) must lead his own family well and see that his children obey him, and he must do so in a manner worthy of full respect. (If anyone does not know how to lead his own family, how can he take care of the church of God?)

Paul teaches us that leadership roles should only be given to those who have the gift of leadership; and that leadership will show up in every area of a person's life. It will not only show up at church, but also at home.

Why is the gift of leadership not placed first in Paul's list in Romans? I think Paul is reminding us that leadership is not about being first; it is about stepping up to help lead those with other gifts to do God's mission. To truly possess the gift of leadership is to be humble and open to leading others to God's promises.

---

11   1 Timothy 3:4-5.

## Ways the gift of Leadership is used

What do leaders do? They can't control people. They can't do everything themselves. Leaders create environments that allow others to do what they are called to do.

This begins with a vision. Whether a leader leads an individual or a group, a leader has an idea about where God wants them to go. Bill Hybels has said that leaders essentially help people move from "here" to "there." The leader has an idea where "there" is. The leader feeds discontent so people understand why they can't stay where they are.

Because a leader can't do everything, he or she must help others win and thrive. In church, the leader helps prophets to bring spiritual energy, servers to meet needs, teachers to deepen the roots, encouragers to bring nourishment, givers to provide generously, and mercy givers to share joy. Those with the gift of leadership think in terms of "team." They understand the body of Jesus is made up of different parts and every part is important. Leaders find joy when they help other people win.

Because leaders help people get from "here" to "there" they have to make decisions. They direct resources and gifts to a certain area in the church, just as a valve directs water in the mainline to certain parts of the orange grove. Leaders know that when they do this, they are using their judgment, guided by the Holy Spirit. They decide that other areas can get by for a while without much attention and be okay. Leaders also understand others will question their judgment. They want to know why everything can't be done at once. That's why those with the Spiritual gift of leadership must spend time in prayer, seeking God's direction. Because all leaders are human beings, they won't hear Jesus correctly all the time. Experience and spiritual growth will help the leader learn how to accurately see what God is doing. Those with the leadership gift always profit when they seek counsel from those who have the prophecy gift.

A leader must decide when to benefit the one and when to protect the many. Jesus told stories about shepherds who faced both responsibilities. When a shepherd with a hundred sheep loses one, he decided the one needs his care and time. He goes searching for that one lost sheep.[12]

But the true leader doesn't focus just on one lamb. Those with leadership gifts understand they are responsible for all of the flock:

> [1]The word of the Lord came to me: [2] "Son of man, prophesy against the shepherds of Israel; prophesy and say to them: 'This is what the Sovereign Lord says: Woe to you shepherds of Israel who only take care of yourselves! Should not shepherds take care of the flock? [3] You eat the curds, clothe yourselves with the wool and slaughter the choice animals, but you do not take care of the flock. [4] You have not strengthened the weak or healed the sick or bound up the injured. You have not brought back the strays or searched for the lost. You have ruled them harshly and brutally. [5] So they were scattered because there was no shepherd, and when they were scattered they became food for all the wild animals. [6] My sheep wandered over all the mountains and on every high hill. They were scattered over the whole earth, and no one searched or looked for them.[13]

---

12  Luke 15:3-7.

13  Ezekiel 34:1-6

The shepherds of Israel were indicted because they didn't care for the whole flock. If you care for the whole flock, you doctor the sick sheep, you keep the flock together, and you don't use the flock for your own benefit.

The ultimate use of the gift of leadership is to help people make the journey God lays before them. The leader helps others use their gifts for the glory of God and to achieve the goals of God.

**You might have the gift of Leadership if:**
- You have followers.
- You can see a future and a purpose for a group of people they have not discovered for themselves.
- You see solutions to problems and others recognize them as the right or best solutions.
- You enjoy accepting responsibility and authority.
- You find yourself taking charge in a group.
- You have a hunger to learn more about leadership.
- You can make decisions not everyone agrees with.
- You have been asked to lead and have helped people get from "here" to "there."

## What to do if you have this gift

If you have the gift of leadership, it is important to understand the Leadership Pipeline.[14] The pipeline looks like this:

### The Leadership Pipeline

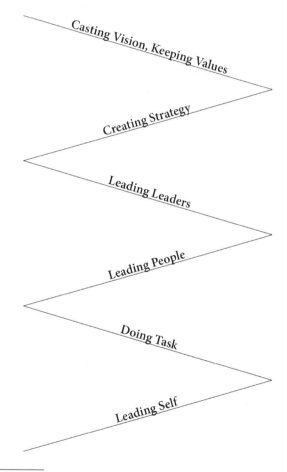

Casting Vision, Keeping Values

Creating Strategy

Leading Leaders

Leading People

Doing Task

Leading Self

14 My version of the Leadership Pipeline is adapted from the book, The Leadership Pipeline, by Ram Charan, Stephen Drotter and James Noel.

The first task of the leader is to lead himself or herself. A leader has to be able to take care of their body, their personal walk with Jesus, get up on time, and be responsible for their own learning. If you have the gift of leadership, begin by leading yourself. On this foundation, everything else will rise or fall.

To grow your leadership, serve. Do tasks. This legitimizes your leadership because you will not ask someone to do what you yourself have not been willing to do if needed. Every great leader serves time as an apprentice, serving the church by doing what needs to be done. I've seen many who want to lead but won't do tasks. They want to tell others what to do – and that's not leadership! That's being a boss. Those who truly have the gift of leadership have proven themselves by serving.

The next step for those with the gift of leadership is to lead people. Seek opportunities to help a group reach a goal. Take on a project. Only by engaging a group will you learn to recognize people's gifts, motivate them to use those gifts, and celebrate with them when their gifts united make something good happen for God.

Often, those who have leadership as a secondary or tertiary gift will find their gift best used at the level of leading people. They excel at working with groups of ten to thirty. This size of group is their sweet spot.

God, however, equips some leaders to move up and lead leaders. At this level on the pipeline the leader is able to help other leaders thrive. Leadership begins to look like coaching. To use the gift of leadership at this level requires maturity, both spiritually and emotionally.

The top legs of the pipeline are strategy and vision. Those with the gift of leadership can see what needs to be done (vision) and they can see how to do it (strategy). Leaders at this level have a God-given sense of what needs to happen; it comes to them. Sometimes the vision takes a while to form; at other times, the vision comes instantly.

I believe those with the gift of leadership should ask God to help them climb as high on the pipeline as He would allow. I've never been in a church that had too many leaders; I've been plenty of churches where people thought they were leaders but didn't have the true gift.

Leadership is a gift that takes time to grow. If you have this gift, it may take years to fully develop. By God's grace, your gift may grow very quickly, but you will need to spend time on every leg of the leadership pipeline to be a fully developed leader.

As Peter Drucker said, the true test of any leader is to check behind himself or herself and find out if anyone is following. If not, you're not a leader. It may be that your gift is not developed. It may be that you trying to lead out of human resources instead of spiritual power. It may be you are simply not a leader, but you want to be one. I find leadership to be a gift that is envied. It has the appearance of power, which is attractive. Those who have the true gift of leadership, however, do not seek power for its own sake; they seek the power of God so they can properly guide people to God's will and purpose for their lives.

Leaders, as I've already said, get frustrated because they cannot control others. You can create the right environment, but people are still free moral agents. They sin. They make poor choices. They rebel. Leaders feel responsible, but for their own mental and spiritual health they must remember they are responsible for doing what God says and for their using their own leadership gifts. Others are responsible for their choices and their obedience to God. Joshua understood this when he told the people of Israel:

> [15] But if serving the Lord seems undesirable to you, then choose for yourselves this day whom you will serve, whether the gods your ancestors served beyond the Euphrates, or the gods of the Amorites, in whose land you are living. But as for me and my household, we will serve the Lord."[15]

The leader leads, but everyone is responsible for their spiritual decisions.

Like a valve shuts water off in one direction so it can flow to another, those with the gift of leadership must learn to say "no" so a "yes" can flow in a different direction. Leaders must say "no" to people who want to hijack a group and make their personal platform for their needs. Leaders must say "no" to people who offer a competing vision for a church or an organization. Leaders must say "no" to people who cannot lead themselves, but know all the answers to the problems of a church or a group of Jesus followers.

The larger a church is, the greater its need for people with the leadership gift. They will lead ministry organizations that support the mission of the church. They lead mission teams. They lead teams that reach out to first time guests. They lead groups that may be taught by others. They lead praise teams that lead the church in worship.

If you have the gift of leadership, take on small problems and solve them. Lead smaller teams to success. Let the visionaries and the strategists learn they can trust you.

---

15   Joshua 24:15.

The gift of leadership does not imply being paid for ministry or serving on the church staff. The New Testament never draws a line between those paid by offerings and those who are paid through outside work. All are servants of Christ. If someone has the leadership gift, it should be used for the sake of Jesus and his church.

## What this gift looks like in real life

John Wooden, the great UCLA basketball coach, had the gift of leadership. A devoted follower of Jesus, he built his basketball teams on what he called "The Pyramid of Success," which outlined his values and beliefs about success, teamwork, and life.[16] At the heart of John Wooden's approach was a deep care for his players. He wanted them to succeed not just on the basketball court, but in all of life. He created an environment that helped his players do their best. Unlike so many coaches, he recognized he was no longer a player, but a coach. He had a different role, not to play the game himself, but to help others play the game better. Though Coach Wooden never expressed it this way, his coaching was his service to Jesus. His mission field was the world of basketball. He was a valve that brought life-giving water to thirsty souls.

My friend, Dick, is one of the best leaders I've ever known. A pastor, who had the skills to be a very successful leader in any field, he brought his gift to God's church. Serving his church for over thirty years, he has helped them achieve more than they could have ever dreamed or imagined. Dick loves meeting with groups, helping them solve problems, and dreaming of what could be. He sees the big picture of the

---

16  See John Wooden and Jay Carty, <u>Coach Wooden's Pyramid of Success.</u>

flock and all its intricacies. Dick's gift of leadership has opened the door for thousands to find the life-giving water of Jesus.

One last leader I'd like you to meet: in the corporate world, Kathy managed multi-million dollar budgets and hundreds of people. In a difficult industry, she was known as the person who would straighten out a problem division and get people on the same page. But Kathy sensed God wanted more for her gifts. She lead small groups at her church and found a fulfillment there she never found in the corporate world. When a job opened at her church, she decided to risk the pay cut and step out in faith. She applied for the position and got it. Her gift of leadership is flourishing because it finally has a stage big enough to hold it. Leadership applied just to dollars quickly becomes limited. Leadership gifts put into an eternal framework know no limits. Kathy is now one of God's valves, putting the life giving water of Jesus just where it needs to go.

## Where from here

Maybe you already know you have the gift of leadership. Find where you are on the Leadership Pipeline. Then pray that God will let you move up the pipeline. The Kingdom needs your gift to grow.

If you just became aware of your gift of leadership, start with self-leadership. What area of your life needs to be straightened up? Lead yourself well. Do the work of a servant, even if you don't have the gift of service. Serving is preparing for a greater work ahead.

God's people need wise leaders who can direct the resources of Jesus to the most desperate needs. Start leading!

# CHAPTER 8

# Sprinkler Pipes: Mercy

When the orange groves were irrigated in my childhood, before micro-jets were placed under each tree, pipes were laid from the well to form a mainline. A valve was attached to direct the water down to a set of pipes that were laid in the middle of a row of trees. This row of pipes contained thousands of tiny holes. We called them "Sprinkler Pipes." As pressure built in the pipe, water would be forced up through the holes and a rain shower would erupt. The life-giving water had returned.

I loved it when my uncles would take me to the end of a row of sprinkler pipes before the valve opened. A shout from the mainline would tell them the water was coming. You could hear the water flooding the pipes, and the pipes would start to strain against their couplings. Then as water filled the pipe, and the pressure rose, baby streams of water would spout. But the pressure would build and soon those streams towered eight to ten feet high. Water would be streaming down the inside of the tree canopy. A dusty row now had water pooling and trickling. You could almost see the ground turn from dry soil to moisture holding mud. I can remember Uncle Dow saying, "It's a mercy we've got irrigation." He remembered days of drought when all a grower could do would be to watch his trees die.

The gift of mercy is like a sprinkler pipe. It streams the grace of Jesus to drought stricken lives. Unlike other gifts that put the water in a very specific place, the gift of mercy is best understood as a flood. Like sprinkler pipes, mercy in abundance transforms multiple lives at once.

## What is Mercy?

Mercy is the final gift in Paul's list. This final gift also is modified by a descriptor. Instead of simply exhorting people to prophesy with their gift of prophecy, Paul has told those who give, to give generously, and for those who lead, to lead with diligent energy. If your gift is mercy, this is his instruction:

> [8d]if it is to show mercy, do it cheerfully.[1]

The Greek word translated "show mercy" is *eleon*, from the word *eleeo*. It means to react to someone who has an affliction and to show them mercy. The word was often used in the realm of justice. Those accused of a crime sought to arouse the emotion of mercy from the judge. Stoic philosophers, contemporaries of Paul, did not hold a high opinion of mercy. They thought it was a sickness of the soul, an unworthy emotion for the wise man. They did not connect mercy to the relational world; they only saw it as an emotion that inhibited impartiality.[2]

From the Old Testament, came the idea that mercy was a favorable quality. It was modeled by God. God himself gives testimony that mercy is central to his character:

---

1  Romans 12:8d.

2  The Theological Dictionary of the New Testament, Vol. II, pp. 477-478.

[6] And the LORD passed before him (Moses) calling, "The Lord, the Lord, compassionate and gracious; slow to anger, and great in mercy and love.[3]

Because God is mercy, over and over his mercy is extended to his people, though they rebelled and sinned. The gift of mercy is associated with the heart of God's character: compassionate, gracious, patient, merciful, and loving.

People with the gift of mercy extend undeserved kindness and care to those in need. This is what God does. Our sin and brokenness creates a crisis, and God responds with mercy. People with the gift of mercy respond to the crisis sin and brokenness created by moving toward the pain and problem, not away from it.

Those with the gift of mercy are instructed to offer the gift with cheerfulness. This is the Greek word *ilaroteti*. It means "glad, merry, or cheerful." The word also appears in 2 Corinthians 9:7, where Paul reminds the Corinthians, "God loves a cheerful giver." Both the gift of giving and the gift of mercy come from an inner generosity. Having received the abundant grace of God, people with the gift of mercy have an inner freedom to be merciful just as God has been merciful to them.[4]

The gift of mercy is moving toward those who suffer adversity and offering them compassion with a heart that knows the mercy of God and thus has been set free to share.

## Biblical Examples of the Gift of Mercy

---

3 Exodus 34:6, author's translation.

4 The Theological Dictionary of the New Testament, Vol. III pp. 297-299.

In the Bible, God is seen as the most merciful character. People in crisis ask him for mercy; he is described as granting that mercy because of his grace. Biblical writers had an overwhelming respect for God and this central part of his character. They preferred to emphasize God's mercy instead of mercy extended from one human being to another.

Jesus gave us two stories that illustrate mercy. The first story perfectly captures a merciful response to a crisis:

[25] On one occasion an expert in the law stood up to test Jesus. "Teacher," he asked, "what must I do to inherit eternal life?"

[26] "What is written in the Law?" he replied. "How do you read it?"

[27] He answered, "'Love the Lord your God with all your heart and with all your soul and with all your strength and with all your mind'; and, 'Love your neighbor as yourself.'"

[28] "You have answered correctly," Jesus replied. "Do this and you will live."

[29] But he wanted to justify himself, so he asked Jesus, "And who is my neighbor?"

[30] In reply Jesus said: "A man was going down from Jerusalem to Jericho, when he was attacked by robbers. They stripped him of his clothes, beat him and went away, leaving him half dead. [31] A priest happened to be going down the same road, and when he saw the man, he passed by on the other side. [32] So too, a Levite, when he came to the place and saw him, passed by on the other

side. [33] But a Samaritan, as he traveled, came where the man was; and when he saw him, he took pity on him. [34] He went to him and bandaged his wounds, pouring on oil and wine. Then he put the man on his own donkey, brought him to an inn and took care of him. [35] The next day he took out two denarii and gave them to the innkeeper. 'Look after him,' he said, 'and when I return, I will reimburse you for any extra expense you may have.'

[36] "Which of these three do you think was a neighbor to the man who fell into the hands of robbers?"

[37] The expert in the law replied, "The one who had mercy on him."

Jesus told him, "Go and do likewise."[5]

Jesus grounds the gift of mercy in a love for God. Unless the love of God has deeply penetrated a person's soul, the gift of mercy remains either inactive or constricted. Love for God leads to loving those around you, neighbors.

In the parable of the Good Samaritan, a traveler is attacked, robbed and left. This man is in crisis. It is the Samaritan who responds to the crisis. Jesus says he took pity on him. The Samaritan's heart was moved. Clarence Jordan thought the Samaritan was saying something like this: "They beat you; they beat me too. They robbed you; they robbed me too. They leave you to die; they've left me to die too. We have got to help each other." Merciful people see what needs to be done and they do it because they themselves have received mercy.

---

5  Luke 10:25-37.

The Samaritan took care of the traveler's wounds, interrupted his schedule to care for him, and paid for his care. Merciful people enter fully into the world of those in crisis.

After Jesus tells this story, the expert in the law must admit the Samaritan was merciful. Mercy can always be recognized because people with this gift engage the problem, the crisis.

Jesus told another story about mercy. This includes an example of great mercy and great callousness:

> [23] "Therefore, the kingdom of heaven is like a king who wanted to settle accounts with his servants. [24] As he began the settlement, a man who owed him ten thousand bags of gold was brought to him. [25] Since he was not able to pay, the master ordered that he and his wife and his children and all that he had be sold to repay the debt.

> [26] "At this the servant fell on his knees before him. 'Be patient with me,' he begged, 'and I will pay back everything.' [27] The servant's master took pity on him, canceled the debt and let him go.

> [28] "But when that servant went out, he found one of his fellow servants who owed him a hundred silver coins. He grabbed him and began to choke him. 'Pay back what you owe me!' he demanded.

> [29] "His fellow servant fell to his knees and begged him, 'Be patient with me, and I will pay it back.'

[30] "But he refused. Instead, he went off and had the man thrown into prison until he could pay the debt. [31] When the other servants saw what had happened, they were outraged and went and told their master everything that had happened.

[32] "Then the master called the servant in. 'You wicked servant,' he said, 'I canceled all that debt of yours because you begged me to. [33] Shouldn't you have had mercy on your fellow servant just as I had on you?' [34] In anger his master handed him over to the jailers to be tortured, until he should pay back all he owed.

[35] "This is how my heavenly Father will treat each of you unless you forgive your brother or sister from your heart."[6]

Debt creates a crisis. The first servant pleads for patience. Like most poor financial managers, he believes he just needs a little more time and he can do the impossible. The master has mercy on him. How rich the master must be to forgive such a great debt! Jesus is telling us the greater the power we have, the greater the wealth we have, the greater the importance of mercy in our lives.

The mercy of the master, however, did not penetrate the servant's heart. Encountering another servant who owed him a reasonable sum of money (think of a hundred days of your salary), the first servant demands immediate repayment. The first servant is not merciful and throws the man in prison until the debt is paid. The master hears of it and withdraws his mercy and the first servant is thrown in prison until the impossible debt is paid.

---

6  Matthew 18:23-35.

The application for people with the gift of mercy is to never be played for the fool. People will take advantage of those with mercy. I can imagine the master felt cheerful when he forgave the large debt. He was living out the instruction to be cheerfully merciful. But when the first servant acted shamefully, the cheerfulness went away. Those with the gift of mercy must be aware of their joy in showing mercy. Only then can their gift be properly shared.

Jesus' stories about mercy teach us that merciful people move toward pain and toward the problems. Because they have received mercy, they give mercy. They extend care, invest in people, but also keep an eye on their joy. When the joy begins to go away, merciful people know the relationship has turned toxic and must be modified.

## Ways the gift of Mercy is used

Merciful people are the people you want to talk to in a crisis. They instinctively know what to say and what not to say. They have high empathy and are usually highly intuitive. Often they sense the true feelings of a person before the person is able to name the feelings themselves. Merciful people excel at empathetic ministry.

Merciful people are outstanding counselors. They receive a person's or a family's crisis and they can hold it without trying to fix it. They can create a safe environment that helps people explore their inner world and come to new understandings of themselves.

Often I meet people who tell me they want to be counselors. When I ask why, they reply, "Because I like to help people and tell them what to do." These people do not have the gift of mercy. More likely they have the gift of prophecy or teaching. The gift of mercy does not "tell;" it "sits with."

In our culture, counseling is seen as a profession. The gift of mercy, however, is not limited to professional counselors. People can deploy this gift by caring for those in need, in Jesus' name. In fact, those who use this gift are able to have significant impact because they are not being paid for the use of their gift.

In our church, deacons visit our local hospital every day. Through the years, I've learned deacon visits have a greater impact than my visits. When I come into a hospital room, people are glad to see me, but the unspoken question is: "Are you here because you care, or are you here because you're paid?" People know the deacon's visit is an act of mercy, freely given.

Many churches train volunteers to counsel with people in basic life situations. I've seen churches who train volunteers to stay at the front after a service to pray for people. These merciful people share their gift with those who come to church carrying burdens. Burdened people are looking for hope and merciful people provide it. Sometimes the counseling is done through support groups. Merciful people can excel at guiding support groups for divorce, grief, addiction issues, and encouragement for deployed military spouses.

Merciful people thrive in crisis ministry. When a hurricane or an ice storm strikes, people need ministries of service, but they also need ministries of mercy. They need to talk with someone to process their grief over the loss of life, of home, and of stability. Merciful people can be with them in their pain.

Certain life stages are tumultuous. People need a merciful presence. Merciful people can be with children who are asking tough questions; they can relate to students who are full of hormones; and they can help senior adults through loss of independence. Merciful ministry can be done in a structured setting, such as leading a group. For example, leading a group of high-schoolers is less about teaching them and more about being with them. Likewise, parents with young children need a merciful environment that encourages them and helps them know they are not alone. But merciful ministry can also be done one on one, such as visiting senior adults who are homebound or who are in nursing homes. They need to know someone understands; a person with the gift of mercy does.

There are people who face a chronic issue that will not go away. They have a loved one who is suffering from Alzheimer's disease; they received a diagnosis of incurable cancer; they suffer with chronic pain; they must care for a profoundly handicapped child. The chronic crisis is exhausting and draining. People with the gift of mercy can come alongside, listen, soothe, and comfort.

My mother suffered with Alzheimer's disease for fifteen years. For the last seven years, she was bed-bound. My step-father, Lawrence, felt the fatigue of her constant care. Thankfully, there were people from their church with the gift of mercy who regularly visited him. They would talk to my mother though she showed no signs of recognition. But most of all they cared for Lawrence. They knew he was not a man to share feelings, but their presence was a signal they understood how difficult it was to live each day with someone you love dying by inches in the next room.

Poverty is a chronic crisis. Lack of education, opportunity, and role models doom some to be caught in a cycle of learned helplessness. Over and over, the Bible instructs us to care for the poor. This means not only meeting their needs, but showing them mercy, being with them in their shame and anger.

Showing mercy to the poor is a reminder that not all crises involve grief or sadness. People with the true gift of mercy can be with people who have emotions of shame, or fear, or anger. They have a wide emotional range.

While other pipes bring the water and guide the water, mercy is a frontline ministry. It meets needy people where they are and brings them the hope of Jesus.

## You might have the gift of Mercy if:

- You are drawn to hurting people.
- You are energized by being with suffering people.
- You respond to those who have created their own problems with compassion instead of judgment.
- You are able to listen to feelings without having to own them or feel responsible for them.
- You find yourself talking with people and offering support during a crisis while you try to help meet their needs.
- You feel drawn toward the sick, the elderly, the disabled, and the needy.
- You are drawn to emotions, not frightened by them.
- You have a high degree of empathy.
- You like to learn about how people think and feel.

## What to do if you have this gift

If you have the gift of mercy, begin by growing your emotional intelligence. Emotions are God's cues to us that something is going on. When someone reacts emotionally, they are telling us something about their world and their understanding of it. Emotional responses are seldom neutral. They evoke an emotional response from the person listening. A merciful person must not only understand the emotions of others, but their own emotional response.

For example, a merciful person may be very comfortable as someone shares the pain of grief. But if the merciful person grew up in a family that was saturated with anger, they may brace against someone else's anger and be unable to offer mercy.

One of the best ways to grow emotional intelligence is to experience merciful counseling yourself. When you experience your feelings being accepted and understood, you are able then to no longer react, but understand the feelings of others. Again, this illustrates the basic truth of the mercy gift: mercy is given after mercy is received.

Merciful people can experience this kind of acceptance and grace through consistent time with God. The command to, "Be still and know that I am God,"[7] is a call for the merciful person to be in God's presence and have his non-judgmental care flow into them.

As emotional intelligence increases, the person with mercy is able to regulate their emotions and thus is able to choose appropriate emotional responses to situations that arise. Both awareness and regulation of emotion means responses can be measured. For example, when

---

7   Psalm 46:10.

a merciful person, who is emotionally aware, approaches someone in grief, they are able to share a nuanced response based on what the person in grief needs, not based on what the merciful person wants to give.

Those with the gift of mercy must grow their heart. God is the preeminent merciful personality in the Bible; his heart is infinite. Growing our hearts means asking God to expand our capacity to care. It means we spend time studying God's responses in scripture to people in crisis. It means we ask God to fill up our own emptiness.

If you have the gift of mercy, you probably already are sharing mercy with others. Find a systematic way to share your gift. Analyze what kind of people touch your heart. Maybe you are drawn to children. Maybe you are drawn to the elderly. Maybe you have a heart for families with special needs. Work within those specific people and share your gift of mercy.

Those with the gift of mercy are uniquely equipped to hear confession. While Protestants think of confession as a Roman Catholic practice, the truth is, we all need to confess our sins:

> [16] Therefore confess your sins to each other and pray for each other so that you may be healed. The prayer of a righteous person is powerful and effective.[8]

Confession, so the saying goes, is good for the soul. To speak aloud our faults and flaws and have them received is grace. Our souls hunger for this grace. People with mercy are able to give grace. They can hear

---

8  James 5:16.

the confession of sin, regulate their response, and offer not judgment but understanding.

There is a 24/7 aspect of mercy. People with this gift find it hard to step away from those in need. If you have this gift, you understand Proverbs 17:17:

> [17] A friend loves at all times,
>   and a brother is born for a time of adversity.

Adversity seldom respects business hours. If you have the gift of mercy, be prepared for late night calls, emergencies, and crisis.

This constant feeling of being "on" means it is essential for the merciful person to monitor each relationship for joy. The instruction of Paul was to use this gift cheerfully. This means you pay attention to any joy drain. Like the parable of the Unmerciful Servant, when cheerfulness begins to go away, it is a sign that it is time to draw a boundary. This does not refer to momentary difficulties or fatigue. Rather, Paul is warning us not to be enablers. This is the temptation of the merciful person. They think if they try a little harder, invest a little more, the person will finally get it.

This is not the way Jesus modeled mercy. He extended grace, but he never enabled. That is why he required faith to be present when he did a miracle. Jesus does the bulk of the work, but he requires our participation and our faith.

Granted, there are times when a person may not be able to do anything. But if you are showing mercy to someone and you are doing all the work emotionally, that is a warning sign. That person needs mercy in a different form than empathy. They may need mercy as confrontation: "this is reality and this is your part of moving forward."

Through the years, I've had a number of parents come to me when their adult children ran afoul of the law. The stories have common features. The adult child has problems, gets in trouble with the law and the parent bails them out. The parent pays off the debt. The parent is doing all the work. Many of these parents have the gift of mercy, but mercy is being applied in a destructive way. The most merciful thing these parents can do is set a boundary. There will be confrontation. The adult child must be forced to face the consequences of his or her choices. This is hard, but it is the most merciful choice for a parent of an adult irresponsible child.

When the cheerfulness of a merciful person goes away, someone else needs to minister to this person or to this situation.

If you have the gift of mercy, grow your emotional intelligence and monitor your joy. Use your gift for those whose lives are shriveling up.

## What this gift looks like in real life

My friend Ed has the gift of mercy. A counselor by trade, he is able to be with people who are in crisis. There is something about being in his presence that is calming. When I visit with Ed, my wife will ask me what we talked about. Many times I have trouble remembering the substance of what Ed says; but I remember the feeling. When I am with Ed, I feel understood; I feel he cares about me; I feel his grace. Every pastor needs a pastor; Ed is my pastor. He is able to embrace the cracks of my soul and be merciful to me.

My friend Kathy has the gift of mercy. She also has the gift of leadership, as I shared in the last chapter. She is that rare person who is able to lead and care. I've seen people drawn to her because she does not judge. I often find myself wondering how she can do it; having the gift of prophecy, judgment comes pretty naturally to me! But she reaches out and shows mercy.

Connie has this gift. She works with students at her church and constantly frets over her lesson. Students, however, do not come to her group to learn; they come because she is merciful. She cares for them and it shows. I've been in her group and the students lean toward her, knowing they will find grace, acceptance, and understanding. What they experience in her group matters more than the information they receive.

### Where from here

If you have the gift of mercy, go toward the hurting, the sad, the depressed, and the ones in crisis. Make sure you are daily receiving the mercy of God and then let it rain out of your soul.

Find the people group God is calling you toward. Grow your emotional intelligence. Find the platform that allows you to be with your group of hurting people.

This world is full of hurting people. Their hurt causes pain unimaginable. Be the rain of grace for them.

CHAPTER 9

# Questions and Answers About Spiritual Gifts

### How do I discover my spiritual gifts?

Rick Warren tells about taking a spiritual gifts inventory and discovering, according to the test, he only had one spiritual gift: martyrdom. To add to his disappointment, he realized his gift was one that could only be used once!

The best way to discover your gifts is to ask God to show you what they are. While reading this book, you probably experienced an "aha!" moment. You read about a gift and thought, "that's me."

Nevertheless, we have included at the end of this book a simple spiritual gifts inventory. The results you get are not the same as a revelation from God, but it may help you to understand yourself.

### The inventory shows I have more than one gift. What does that mean?

Most people have more than one spiritual gift. God gives people different combinations to do their specific purpose in life.

Some combinations are common. Prophecy and teaching gifts are often paired. People with the gift of mercy often have the gift of encouragement. The gift of service is often joined with encouragement or giving.

Most often three gifts show up strongly in a person's life. For example, my three strongest gifts are prophecy, teaching, and leadership. At different seasons of my life, one of the gifts will show stronger. This is probably because of the challenge I'm facing at that moment. But there is no question my three gift combo is ideal gifting for a pastor. God has equipped me for what he wants me to do.

Another common triad is service, giving, and mercy. These are people who love to help and feel compassion for those they help. People with the triad of service, encouragement, and mercy excel at people-centered ministry instead of task-centered ministry.

The triad of service, encouragement, and leadership is perfect for those who are called to lead from the second chair. They may not be at the top of the organization, but they are heading up a key ministry or a key area. Their people-oriented gifts help soothe the rough edges of prophetic leader.

### I don't have three strong gifts. In fact, I seem to have some of all of them. What does that mean?

If you take the inventory and seem to have a smattering of all the gifts, it means one of two things.

First, it may mean God has equipped you as a multi-purpose player. Every baseball team needs a utility infielder – someone who can play each position in the infield. This versatile player is insurance. If anyone goes down, he can step up.

I've noticed people with some proportion of all the gifts are often called to serve as missionaries. To be a missionary is to enter a hostile culture and challenge that culture with the Gospel. Because the church in this hostile culture will not be strong, the leaders often have to have all the gifts until such a time as other Jesus followers grow their gifts and use them.

The second thing your inventory may indicate is reluctance on your part to embrace who God has made you to be. The temptation on the inventory is to give the response you think is right, not the response that best describes you. For example, I would rather talk to someone about faith than set up chairs. Yet something inside of me resists telling the truth about this. I think it is the voice of my step-father Lawrence, who had the gift of service. He would rather set up chairs than talk and taught me setting up chairs was more virtuous. It's not.

If your inventory shows a mixture of all the gifts, I would encourage you to wait a day, retake the test (which can also be found at alicedrive. org), and answer out of your preference, not out of your guilt.

### I have the opposite problem. On several of the gifts, I score nothing! Does this mean I don't have to do those things?

Absolutely not! For example, whenever I take the inventory I score either a zero or a one for the gift of giving. Does this mean I am off the hook when it comes to giving? Of course not!

Some of the gifts are required of all followers of Jesus. We are all commanded to serve, to encourage, to give, and to be merciful. If these are not in your gift mix, it means you do them to fulfill your obligation to Jesus. You probably will not feel the same joy as someone with the gift, but these become spiritual disciplines you do so your soul can be reshaped.

I discovered over the years, giving is changing my soul. Because I have the gift of prophecy, it is easy for me to judge. To do so outside of God's leadership is to sin. Giving makes me more selfless and in turn, makes me more merciful. What is a gift for some is a spiritual discipline for me.

The gifts of prophecy, teaching, and leadership are more specific and are not required for everyone. If these are not in your gift mix, don't worry about acquiring them.

### Can I ask for a gift?
Sure! But you have to trust what God gives you, and accept His role for you. Do not waste time envying the gift you don't have.

### Which Spiritual Gifts did Jesus have?
The Bible never actually tells us which gifts Jesus had. However, because Jesus was God, it is safe to assume that he had all the gifts and had a full measure of all the gifts.

Jesus prophesied: He told people that God was doing something new, that the Kingdom was at hand. Jesus served: one night He took a basin and washed His disciple's feet. Jesus taught: the Sermon on the Mount, the parables He shared, and the lessons He explained to the disciples were all the times He used this gift. Jesus encouraged others: he encouraged the disciples to no longer see themselves as fishermen, but as fishers of men. Jesus gave: though a poor man, He provided food for over 5,000 men, plus women and children. Jesus led: He gave His disciples a vision of what could be and a mission statement that has stood the test of time (Go, make disciples, baptizing them...). Jesus showed mercy: He died for us on the cross so our sins would not take our souls to death.

Whatever your gifting may be, Jesus knows what it is to have and use that gift. He understands the unique burdens and challenges you will face.

## How do I put my gifts to use?

Don't wait to be asked! Chances are you already feel a tug to use your gifts. When you use them, you feel energy.

People often ask me to help them find their purpose. I get the feeling they want me to give them a job or a ministry responsibility. The truth is I can only suggest and guide. Ultimately the responsibility of using your gift rests on you.

If you have trouble knowing what to do, initiate a conversation with a pastor or a staff member at church. Try a ministry. If it's not a fit, that's okay. Accept that you found one thing not to do and try something else. Most people experience stops and starts along the way as they discover the calling that matches their gifts.

Some churches have a staff person who functions as the volunteer Human Resources Coordinator. Talk to that person about opportunities for you.

If your calling and your gifting requires a ministry platform your church doesn't have, join an organization that provides that opportunity. For example, several people in our church are gifted and called to natural disaster crisis ministry. We don't offer that, but our state organization does. They serve the cause of Jesus there.

If no organization offers what you feel called to and are gifted to do, God may be calling you to start your own ministry. I once met a man who had the gift of prophecy and service, but he hated speaking in front of people. He felt God was calling him to be his pastor's personal prayer warrior. Unknown to anyone, including the pastor, this man's ministry was to pray for the pastor two to three hours a day. That sounds like a valid ministry to me.

In short, never let lack of opportunity keep you from sharing your gifts. God will open the doors you need.

## Do I have to have any of these gifts to be saved?

No! Sometimes when people talk about spiritual gifts, it is implied or overtly stated that one gift is required to give evidence of your salvation. The Bible does not teach this. God will give you at least one of these gifts we've discussed. Your salvation, however, depends on his grace and is shown by his love, not by your spiritual gifts:

[35]By this everyone will know that you are my disciples, if you
love one another.[1]

The proof of our salvation is in our love for each other, not what gift
we have.

### What if I don't have any of the gifts?

It is doubtful you would have no gifts. Even people far from God have
the shadows of spiritual gifts in their talents and abilities. But if you
have no gift at all, I would humbly ask you to pray about this. This
could be an indicator that you have never truly decided to follow Jesus.
Thus, the gifts the Holy Spirit wants to bring to you have never come
upon you.

### Can my gifts change over time?

The Bible doesn't say. My experience is gifting generally remains the
same over time. I think this is required because most of the gifts require time to mature and completely develop. God in his sovereignty
may offer a new gift for a season or a specific occasion for his purpose.
I do not have the gift of healing (which I think is under the heading of
encouragement) but I have prayed for people, laid hands on them, and
they were healed. God granted me that gift for that moment.

### What's the difference between a talent and gift?

A spiritual gift is divinely given and divinely energized. It operates
beyond human power. I experience this when I preach, using the gift
of prophecy. I have a talent for speaking; that was recognized in my
high school speech class. But when I preach, I express thoughts that

---

1 John 13:35.

come from beyond me. I listen to myself and wonder, "Where did that come from?" That isn't talent; it's a gift.

Talents often foreshadow gifts. Talent, however, is not a prerequisite for using the gifts God gives you.

### What about other gifts mentioned in the Bible?

As I shared in the first chapter, I believe Romans 12:6-8 offers us categories of gifts. Other gifts mentioned in scripture can be placed under these gifts. At the end of the book, I've categorized other gifts under these headings. This is merely my opinion and my division should not be considered authoritative, merely suggestive.

### Can I lose my Spiritual Gifts?

The Bible doesn't say. Jesus does tell us the story of talents, however, which offers some insight for us.[2] Three servants were given different amounts of money and were charged with their care. Two servants used what they had been given and multiplied it. They were praised by the master. One servant did nothing with his gift. He presented to the master intact, but unused. The master condemned him for his laziness.

Jesus' point is hard to miss. We are to use what God gives us, not keep it safe. To follow Jesus means having faith. I think Jesus would tell us, "Don't worry about losing your gift; use your gift!"

---

2   Matthew 25:14-30.

### What's the difference discovering your Spiritual Gifts and discovering your Purpose?

The two go hand in hand. Your purpose is what God has designed you uniquely to do. It will involve knowing Jesus, knowing community, growing character, and going and sharing what God has done for you. Your spiritual gifts will help you in each next step. For example, if you have the gift of service, each time you serve, you will know Jesus better; because Jesus was a servant. If you have the gift of mercy, each time you share that gift you know community and connection with others. If you have the gift of giving, each time you give you are growing your character to be like Jesus', because Jesus is a giver. If you have the gift of teaching, each time you teach, you are going and sharing Good News with a thirsty world.

As you use your gifts, your soul is shaped by the Spirit to be more like Jesus. Using spiritual gifts is spiritual formation.

# CHAPTER 10

# Faith in the Well

It's all about the well. You can have a great system of irrigation pipes, with a mainline and valves, micro-jets and sprinklers, but if you don't have a well, you have nothing to put in the pipes.

I know organizations that seek to do a lot of good in the world. Some of them even claim to be Christian in their purpose. They build a system, but at the end of their line of pipes, nothing seems to change. Those organizations never connected to the well.

Jesus is the well. He told a woman at a well one day:

> [13]"Everyone who drinks this water will be thirsty again, [14] but whoever drinks the water I give them will never thirst. Indeed, the water I give them will become in them a spring of water welling up to eternal life."[1]

Ultimately it's not about you. You are the pipe. It is about Jesus. He is the well that puts out the life giving water of God's grace, forgiveness,

---

1   John 4:13-14.

and peace. By His death on the cross, the drought caused by our sin was broken. He brought the life of the ages, eternal life.

This is why Paul began with the idea of faith:

> [6] We have different gifts, according to the grace given to each of us. If your gift is prophesying, then prophesy in accordance with your faith;[2]

All gifts are grace. We don't deserve them. We receive them. But just having the gifts is not enough. They must be energized by our faith.

To have faith in Jesus is to put our confidence in Him, in His teaching, in His saving work on the cross, and in His resurrection that breaks the power of death. Faith in Jesus means we trust Him more than we trust our fears, more than we trust our own strength, more than we trust what we can see. To have faith in Jesus means we rely on Him. If He approves of our work, no other approval is necessary. If He instructs us to take a risk, we believe Him.

To have faith in Jesus is to believe He can do more through us than we do by ourselves.

Every well on earth has limitations. Wells are limited by the size of the pipe that draws the water. They are limited by the horsepower of the motor that drives them. And they are limited by the quantity of water in the underground reservoir they tap.

But Jesus has no limitations. He is limitless in power, in grace, and in capacity. He will always provide more than we can imagine or think:

---

2  Romans 12:6.

[20] Now to him who is able to do immeasurably more than all we ask or imagine, according to his power that is at work within us, [21] to him be glory in the church and in Christ Jesus throughout all generations, for ever and ever! Amen.[3]

What you can do with your gift is not limited, it is limitless. Those who maximize their gifts report the more their gift grows, the more they can see God doing what they never imagined.

For your spiritual gift to be truly used, stay connected to the well. Spend time with Jesus. Talk to Him. Study scripture to learn about Him. Strive to be like Him. Give to Him. Serve Him. Then feel the amazing moments when His grace is pumped out through you and people find hope.

When that happens, it's a good day to be a pipe in God's hands.

I pray that day comes often for you.

---

3  Ephesians 3:20-21

# Spiritual Gifts Survey

## Discovering Your Spiritual Gifts

**DISCOVERING YOUR GOD-GIVEN GIFTS.** Here is a simple test to help you identify some of your special gifts. It focuses on seven ministry gifts that are mentioned in Romans 12:6-8.

For each question, choose the response which best describes you. Then tabulate your scores. (Ignore letters in front of responses until the exercise has been completed).

*"We have different gifts, according to the grace given us. If a man's gift is prophesying, let him teach; if it is encouraging, let him encourage; if it is contributing to the needs of others, let him give generously; if it is leadership, let him govern diligently; if it is showing mercy, let him do it cheerfully."* Romans 12:6-8

**Would you consider it more loving and caring to:**
P ____ help a person change for the better
S ____ invite a needy person into your home

**Would you rather:**
T ____ train others to do a job
A ____ delegate work to others

**To form an opinion about something, would you:**

P ＿＿＿ go by what you feel and believe already

T ＿＿＿ research it until you are confident enough

**Would you rather spend time:**

P ＿＿＿ in prayer

A ＿＿＿ organizing a Christian project

**In giving advice, do you:**

P ＿＿＿ quote Scripture as basic ideal for action

E ＿＿＿ give practical, motivational steps for action

**Do you find that you:**

T ＿＿＿ enjoy intellectual pursuits

C ＿＿＿ daydream and fantasize a lot

**Are you more likely to find fulfillment in a:**

T ＿＿＿ Teaching career

G ＿＿＿ Business venture

**Would you rather participate in:**

P ＿＿＿ an intercessory prayer group

A ＿＿＿ a program to feed the poor

**Would you rather:**

P ＿＿＿ pray for someone

G ＿＿＿ provide for him/her

**Would you prefer to:**

E ＿＿＿ do individual counseling

A ＿＿＿ manage a group project

**Would you rather:**

S ＿＿ help set up for and serve at a church dinner

T ＿＿ speak to the group after dinner

**Do you encourage people:**

E ＿＿ by sharing your own experiences

G ＿＿ by giving them practical help

**Would you rather encourage people to:**

G ＿＿ give generously to a ministry

C ＿＿ minister directly to those who are hurting

**Would you rather:**

E ＿＿ give motivational speeches

C ＿＿ help with caring-type ministries

**If a room needed cleaning, would you:**

S ＿＿ get a broom and sweep it yourself

A ＿＿ figure out who is best suited for the job

**After a meeting do you feel it is more important to:**

S ＿＿ make sure the room is left in order

E ＿＿ spend time socializing

**Would you rather work with:**

A ＿＿ a group

C ＿＿ one person at a time

**Would you rather:**

G ＿＿ financially assist an ongoing project

A ＿＿ organize the ongoing project

**Are you more attentive to:**

S ___ people's practical needs

C ___ how people feel

**Would you rather help someone in need by:**

S ___ doing something for him/her

G ___ anonymously giving money

**Do you like to have:**

T ___ a few select friends with similar interests

E ___ lots of friends, the more the better

---

Review the answers you checked. Count the number of "A's" and put that number on the line next to Administrator on the next page. Do the same for the other letters/gifts. When you are done, you will have a preliminary idea of what your ministry gifts may be.

# Learn More About Your Spiritual Gifts

Please transfer your scores from the previous pages to this page for your personal records.

_____ Administrator          _____ Compassion Person

_____ Encourager             _____ Giver

_____ Prophecy               _____ Server

_____ Teacher

**Administrator/Leader**: The God-given ability to know how a ministry functions, create plans for a ministry, and implement procedures that accomplish the goals of that ministry.

**Encourager**: The God-given ability to reassure people who are discouraged or wavering in their faith.

**Prophecy**: The God-given ability to discern and boldly reveal truth that rebukes, corrects, and edifies believers and leads to life change and/or repentance.

**Teacher**: The God-given ability to grasp the truth of God's Word, help others understand its meaning, and motivate them to apply what has been learned.

**Compassion**: The God-given ability to joyfully meet the emotional and practical needs of those who are suffering.

**Server**: The God-given ability to joyfully accomplish practical tasks that support a ministry or person.

**Giver**: the God-given ability to unselfishly give money and resources to individuals in need and to the work of the church.

## Facts about Spiritual Gifts:

- Every member has at least one spiritual gift, usually two or three.
- Every member should be using his or her gifts to serve others through the church.
- No member has all the gifts, so we need each other.
- No gift is given to all members. God decides who receives which gift.

**We are most fulfilled when we are serving in our area of giftedness through God's Church – utilizing our gifts for His glory. [1]**

---

1 This instrument was originally taken from a study on Spiritual Gifts that is now out of print. Alice Drive Baptist Church has used it through the years and we have misplaced the original. We regret that we cannot properly attribute it to its source and promise we will make corrections in future editions.

# Gift Categories

| Category: | Other Gifts: |
| --- | --- |
| Prophecy | Speaking in Tongues, Interpreting Tongues, Discernment, Faith |
| Service | Hospitality, Helps, Celibacy |
| Teaching | Knowledge, Wisdom |
| Encouragement | Miracles, Evangelism, Martyrdom, Voluntary Poverty |
| Giving | |
| Leadership | Apostleship, Administration, Pastor |
| Mercy | Healing |

# Acknowledgments

First, my thanks to Alice Drive Baptist Church for making this book possible.

Second, thank you to Myra Yeatts who did the bulk of editing in this book. Her suggestions were invaluable, needed, and make this a much better book. Also thank you to Abram Smith as always for his insights and suggestions. All the errors of fact and writing are mine. Thank you to the readers for your patience and indulgence.

Thank you to Laurie Hussey, my assistant who helped me to chase down things I need to know. She kept my calendar shuffled so I could get this book finished.

Thank you to Nancy Lee Zimpleman, who did the legwork in getting this book from electrons to paper and bargained with the publisher for extra time.

Thank you to Matthew Morse for his help in compiling the chapters in a coherent book and for his brilliant cover design.

All citations of scripture in this book are from the New International Version, copyright, 2011, except where otherwise noted.

## Acknowledgments

Thank you to my cousin Ned Hancock, who knows more about orange groves than any man I know. Most of the insights about irrigation and orange production can be traced to conversations I've had with him over the years.

Finally, thank you to Gina Smith, my wife, who encourages me, helps me find space and time to write, and gives me grace. She is a woman with great gifts of encouragement and mercy. I'm grateful she shares those gifts with me. There are not enough words to express my debt to her.

# Author's Biography

William Clay Smith has served for over twenty years as pastor of Alice Drive Baptist Church in Sumter, South Carolina. He also served churches in Florida and Kentucky. A graduate of Samford University, he obtained the Doctor of Philosophy degree from The Southern Baptist Theological Seminary in Louisville, Kentucky. He served as an adjunct instructor at Southern Seminary, St. Leo's University, and The University of South Carolina.

He is married to Gina, a counselor in Sumter. They have three children: Abram, Hannah, and Sarah.

A native Floridian, his family still owns the orange groves he describes in this book.